BLACK STAR RISING

PETER KALU

Nia

Published in United Kingdom by:
Nia. An imprint of The X Press,
6 Hoxton Square, London N1 6NU
Tel: 0171 729 1199
Fax: 0171 729 1771

Printed by Caledonian International Book Manufacturing Ltd, Glasgow, UK.

Distributed in UK by Turnaround Distribution, Unit 3, Olympia Trading Estate,
Coburg Road, London N22 6TZ
Tel: 0181 829 3000
Fax: 0181 881 5088

ISBN 1-874509-53-0

ABOUT THE AUTHOR

Thirty year old Peter Kalu is the winner of numerous literary prizes including the BBC Young Playwrights Festival. *Black Star Rising* is his third sci-fi book, the previous two, *Lick Shot* and *Professor X* featuring the black futuristic detective Ambrose Patterson, are currently being made into a TV series. He lives in Manchester with his wife and children.

Peter Kalu's body is connected to the first imagination to see space and science fiction through afro-centric eyes. Somewhere in the future, earthlings will look back and say Peter Kalu was the first. Weak hearts beware, there is a dread at the controls.

Benjamin Zephaniah

For Philbert

Five black astronauts crewing one ship was not something that had occurred before. The chances of it happening at random were 1 in 750,263, but Command did not leave such things to random. So why? The crew themselves had not been told. It wasn't as if they looked likely to gel into a particularly effective unit. None of them had won any prizes for teamwork.

Take Officer Kaya, the rocket technician. He was a handsome man in a beaten up kind of way; in his late forties, and within crew template height. He had blue-black skin, shoulder blade length, greying dreadlocks, and a Tutankhamen wave black beard which he was much given to stroking; his voice was an East Way baritone and he wore a turquoise Egyptian scarab ring on his left index finger. Officer Kaya was responsible for maintenance of the ship's four main and fifteen auxiliary jets, for the duration of the tour. Nineteen rockets was plenty for one mechanic on a tour of this length. But the workload didn't faze Kaya. He was a brilliant engineer — always had been. Apprenticed on the rookie finishing ship, Delta Four Raft, Kaya had been fast-streamed into the Zimbabwe Space Force. With his talent, and deep intelligence, he should have risen all the way to Command Control level, indeed would have so risen, but for the one big flaw. Kaya tended to speak his mind too freely. He was a rootsman — raised by his bio-scientist parents on planet Kayiga. Although he had had the full set of softsystems implanted during the newborn ceremony, there survived in his makeup a strong feel for the intuitive, for the free. He'd made several unguarded criticisms of Command Control judgments as a cadet. He was warned, but took no notice. Finally they marked him down as a control risk, and sidelined him into the engineering fleets. On ships such as zsf-e5 Officer Kaya had dutifully served for seventeen tours of one year. Despite his bog mouth, Kaya got on well with the other members of the e5 crew. He touched the human, rather than the soft side of his colleagues. There was a warm rapport between himself and both Officer Triple and Lieutenant Sky. Officer Kaya's aura was early brown.

By contrast, Lieutenant Sky's aura was corn yellow.

Lieutenant Sky was a woman serenely strong of mind, and the oldest of the crew at fifty-six Urth years. As the ship's Communicator she was fluent in fourteen of the seventeen language systems used across the known Cosmos. And those three systems she didn't know she could improvise. As well as Communicator, Sky was Team Physician and Psychologist — the official glue of the crew. On every ship she served, Sky had shown she understood individual crew emotions, often better than the crew understood them themselves. She liked to let them work through their emotional problems, even if it caused temporary disruption of routine. It enabled them to grow as crew and as people. Command had spotted Sky's capacity for 'enablement' and considered it overblown. It was a flaw too major for them to allow her to top grade. So she became engineering stock. Not that she was unhappy to serve there.

Lieutenant Sky was self-aware enough to know she was not leadership material like Captain Mandella. The lieutenant recognised Mandella's leadership aptitude in the natural authority of her Captain's voice. Sky's own voice was the gentle voice of calm, not compulsion; Sky had inherited Nubian looks: tall and lithe, and left-handed (a strange anomaly that last, because they thought they'd gene-programmed it out). Sky had deep, warm green eyes, and clear, middle brown skin.

For all the lieutenant's admiration of Mandella, Sky was troubled by her new Captain's ignorance of the crew's well being. As leader, Captain Mandella ought to have been picking up, as she, Sky was, on their poor emotional state. Kaya was having strange bouts of fantasy. Just two shifts ago he'd declared to her in all earnestness that he was of Royal Rasta bloodline and that he could trace his roots back to the Royal Prophet Robert Nesta Marley, and from there back even further to the cradle Zimbabwe civilisation. Sky had humoured the rocketsman. But he worried her. Then there was young Triple. His aching loneliness. It hurt her to see the boy wandering head down, feet dragging along the corridors during Free. Captain Mandella didn't feel these hurts, it seemed, or else chose not to acknowledge them. Blanking the poor state of the crew's emotional well-being only forced them to store it up as pain, Sky knew. It would break out eventually, worse than if it had been dealt with earlier on. Not three months into the mission, Sky was already seeing Officer Triple's distress show in the iridescence of his pale blue aura.

Officer Triple didn't know Lieutenant Sky was thinking this. Eighteen Urth years old, Triple was the ship's Information Surfer and Gunner. He was a tall, rangy, ambidextrous youth with a terracotta brown face and a gold pirate's earring in his left ear. He was naturally exuberant and bold, optimistic and jokey and often all these things at once and more. Prior to the zsf-e5 assignment, Triple had served only on a Cadets' Virtual Reality Ship — a Vurt.

At times, Officer Triple genuinely loved life on board zsf. It was all new to him, and he was still experimenting. He loved to play LaserBall in the FunRoom. He loved to work out on the Fitness Gyroscope. He loved to jog along the corridors to the cargo bulkheads and back. And he was engrossed by the dreams he experienced in his sleep chamber. The food, well... the best he could say of the food on e5 was that it was novel.

Triple knew he was the 'new kid on the block', and he tried hard to please the others and have them accept him. He got along fine with old man Kaya and his love of Organics. He loved Lieutenant Sky's poise, and her sincere vibe, the way she walked and the way her breasts moved when she... Perhaps he loved the lieutenant more than was healthy for one crew member to love another, but he pushed this thought to one side. He was quietly scared though, of Captain Mandella. The Captain was distant and severe. So far, some three months into the one year tour, he'd damped his natural charisma and tried to impress her with his surf skill. But it was getting to be a chore, this acting like a robot. There were times when he felt so stifled he hated it all — times when he sat down on his bunk in the Sleep Chamber and silently cried himself to sleep.

Triple was not really senior enough to be on a full one year tour. But all the frontline Surfers had been called up to fix a major code foul-up in Amik's Attic and apprentices had had to be promoted before their time. Triple's spatial cognition and reaction speeds were Alpha Star One. And he had never let them down yet. He was immature though. Too young, Triple himself would have said, for such a long tour. Triple could feel a strange mindcold sapping his will.

Then there was Mandella.

Zsf-e5's captain was in her late thirties, heavy-set, and of slightly below template height. Her skin was damson black. She walked with her small nose high, when she walked. Usually, she was to be found standing on the dais of the ship's bridge, alone. She cut a stern and brooding presence on that dais.

Mandella had a thorough grasp of all zsf e5 systems and at a pinch, could do most of the crew's jobs. This was a great consolation to her, because she had serious misgivings about the competence of her crew. She hadn't chosen them. Command had imposed them on her. The first all-black crew she'd captained. That anybody had captained. Why the crew was all black she did not know. And had no authority to ask. She knew they were Beta material. Officer Kaya was analogue. His holistic philosophies annoyed her. She didn't understand how he squared such views with his profession of rocket engineer. And he led Officer Triple astray. Not that that was hard to do. Officer Triple had been an irritation from day one, and she had difficulty hiding it. Wherever he was, the urchin (as she called him to herself) always seemed to take up too much space. His youth was no excuse. She recognised his surfing competence, but that was it, in terms of positives. Of the crew, only Lieutenant Sky passed muster. Her new lieutenant had poise and maturity. Exuded a quiet competence. She was surprised the lieutenant was still marooned in the career backwaters of the engineering fleets. Mandella wished she'd had Sky on her last ship. Lieutenant Sky might have made the difference. The captain relived the disaster of that last ship every time she freedreamed. The colour of Mandella's aura was purple.

The fifth astronaut was the ship's computer. Or, more accurately, computers. Zsf-e5 ran on four identical, parallel computers, each constantly checking and rechecking the others. Inputs came from various surface, embedded and ambient scanners and probes distributed throughout the ship's structure. The Computer controlled all the ship's support systems and membranes. The official name of the Computer was the ForceCode.

In so far as it had an aura, the ForceCode's aura was black. The blackness of space. The blackness of the unknown and the all-knowing. The blackness from which all light emerged. The ForceCode was lawgiver, arbiter and great store of answers. Understandably therefore the crew (which in zsf engineering fleet argot meant all on board bar the Captain), chose to call the Computer 'Omm'.

In normal conditions, the Computer remained in the background, silently observing, interpreting and recording the ship's and crew's actions. Very occasionally, it would spontaneously offer an opinion or override a false setting. But the norm was for it merely to observe and to respond to the crew's enquiries and requests. It was an enabler, not a dictator. Normally.

★

On Day Circadian 121 of their mission the crew were summoned out of their second quarter shift Free by the captain. She knew they would not appreciate being called away from their diversions, and that it was a waste of time since she had already decided what she was going to do, but it was the Procedure to consult the crew first, and she always followed Procedure.

Triple made it first, then Kaya, onto the Bridge, both looking fuzzed and half in, half out of their uniforms, Kaya dripping wet so they had probably been Fastballing. Presently Lieutenant Sky appeared. Mandella had summoned them using First Amber Auditory and they got into groove without chat.

"Officer Kaya, latitude?" requested Captain Mandella.

"Latitude Twenty-Four Point Six, South-South West of Orion nebula, Captain."

"Longitude?"

Kaya checked the charts on his screen. "Longitude unchanged, Captain."

"Engines Alpha One?"

"Engines A One," Kaya confirmed.

"Lieutenant Sky, sensors at normal?"

"The planets are all quiet, Captain" came the reply.

There was a lull.

"So, what's the shout?" Officer Kaya finally called out, stroking his beard into shape. He'd checked his console. Omm had not flagged any on-board technical problem. Planet Thuli and its orbiting space stations were still five days away. There was no space station or craft in the vicinity that might require servicing. Nothing on screen that merited Amber.

"We're closing on Meridian Two," Mandella intoned,

"barely forty-eight hours away. I shouldn't need to remind you that Meridian Two borders on Logos territory."

"Has something shown on the scanners, Captain?" queried Lieutenant Sky.

"Like has there been an intelligence report from Command?" said Triple.

Mandella eyeballed him.

"*Captain*—" he said, "has there been an intelligence report, *Captain?*"

"No."

"Then why the amber, Cap'n?" Kaya said. "You pulled us from a stinker. We were screeching, right brother?" Triple laughed.

Captain Mandella ignored them both.

"Lieutenant Sky, go over identification protocols for Thuli and Logos," she intoned. "It must be clear to any Logos presence that we are a non-hostile service craft with no significant weaponry. Officer Kaya, finetune all rockets in readiness. Officer Triple, practise Object Verification — Specialisation Protocol: Logos fighter craft."

Triple sighed.

Kaya spoke up.

"But with respect Captain, if Logos wants to dust us, they will. We're engineering craft, not a warship, and with no defences worth the name. Even with rockets on maxburn, we're chicken to their fox."

Mandella blanked him. "You have your orders. Execute them."

"And what will you be doing, Captain?" Lieutenant Sky said rising from her seat.

"I'm the Captain. I'll decide that," Mandella riposted. Then cooled. It was a level question. "I'll be working out some evasion routes, in case of trouble. That satisfactory?"

Lieutenant Sky nodded.

Triple shot a glance to Kaya that said, 'What's eating her?'

Kaya shrugged, mimed him to 'keep the vibes sweet', then logged on at Engines with Omm.

Kaya gave the captain the benefit of the doubt. She was after all the Captain. He'd do the retunework, even if it was pointless.

Omm brought to Kaya's screen a rotating, real-time hologram of the ship. He looked at it as it rotated, surprised again at its all-round hideousness. There was no getting away from it — zsf-e5 was an ugly, ramshackle craft, a mauled, matt grey, lozenge-shaped weld of kevlar glass and steel that somebody somewhere in Command Logistics must love irrationally because it should have been scrapped five tours ago. The bridge and the main suite of control rooms were at the bow. To the stern were the sleep chambers, and the pleasure cubicle. Between these areas were three relaxation rooms: one for meditation, one for physical exertion games, and the other for socialising, or flopping as the crew called it. The living craft was dwarfed fifty to one by the supplies hulks it was towing in its wake. There were five separate hulks. They resembled monster carriages of a skyfloating train. On the screen, the lower starboard booster engine Kaya chose highlighted. He clicked again and the hologram zoomed in.

Kaya had chosen the smallest auxiliary engine. The smaller ones were always the trickiest. He'd do those first, while his head was still fresh. Some servicing could be done remotely. Some things you had to spanner. The question that went begging for any engineer responding to the Captain's order was of course, fine-tune for what? It was one matter to finetune for endurance travel, something quite different to fine-tune for the high torgue, missile-avoidance bursts that Mandella seemed to be indicating might be necessary. The latter job was not a finetune, it was a fully fledged retune. Moreover, in their short optimum burst settings, these engines not only suffered high wear but guzzled for up to three times the normal fuel. Which meant a detour after Thuli to refuel with all the delay that involved. Had Captain

Mandella understood this? Kaya often wondered just what she did understand. She had no engineering qualifications that he knew of. He asked Omm for the calibration settings for lower starboard's maximum burst. Omm gave him the settings instantly and he got on with it.

Triple dragged his basketball player's feet along Gunnery Corridor Two. Mandella had told him to not come back until he'd beaten his personal best. Why was she so down on him? He'd be on his own there for three hours. That was how long it would take to get anywhere near his p. b. Anybody else's p. b. he could reach in minutes. But his own... How the gifted suffer, he consoled himself. And tramped on.

The Gunnery was located at the apex of the living craft. Accessible only via a series of corridors, ladders and bulkhead doors, it was a one-person cermet glass bauble, or, as Triple told it, a zit on the bald dome of the living craft. And it had a peashooter for a gun. He'd used more powerful lasers on Cadet Ship. That there was a Gunnery at all, Kaya had told him one time, was thanks only to the Unions. Apparently, there'd been a dispute with Command over sending maintenance crew "all over the Cosmos without even the puniest protection". In the face of a likely work-to-rule, Command had backed down and said they'd fit something appropriate. When it was all costed out, this joke of a gun was what they came up with. Union funds had been too depleted by the last strike to organise another protest so the proposals had been endorsed by the union, subject to review in three years time. Kaya said it was better than nothing. But was it? Sometimes nothing was a smarter play.

Triple got into the bauble, seated himself and strapped down. He glanced at the sky and didn't recognise it. This was one major swerve they were doing. Why had Omm had them swerve so far from the original route to Thuli? He didn't know. You got told shit on this craft. Maybe there was some space warp they were avoiding. He switched on the Vurt simulator, then waited for the phantom projections to appear on the bauble's darkening, cermet glass membrane.

Lieutenant Sky approached Captain Mandella at the dais. "Captain...?" She knew the Captain hated her commands being questioned.

"It's a drill," Mandella came back fast. She had read her lieutenant's impending line of enquiry. She curled her upper lip slightly. "There will be no sloppiness on this ship."

"They have done well so far," Sky said.

Mandella made no response.

"They were on Free. To pitch them out of Free is not routine."

"Danger does not respect routine, Lieutenant."

"Without sufficient Free, they'll burn out long before the tour is over."

Captain Mandella turned to her lieutenant. The briefest wry smile flitted across her face.

"Lieutenant Sky, don't rattle your worrybones. They'll get all the freetime they could wish for, once we've cleared Thuli."

Sky nodded, relieved.

"I'll communicate this to them."

"You do that," said Mandella, "and perhaps now you'll put some work in yourself — like the I.D. protools I asked for, lieutenant? Unless you've not quite finished with me."

"Yes, Captain," she smiled. *"Nitakayefanya "*.

Captain Mandella stayed at the dais. It was one of the truisms of space travel that you got to know your crew on a deep level, whether you wanted to or not. All the rules and routines, all the procedures and protocols invented could not shield you from the fact that at the end of the day, you were a bunch of human beings spending a lot of time with each other in a confined space. A year cooped up in a tiny craft with the same people took a special kind of personality to endure. There was nowhere to hide on a spacecraft, nowhere to wander off and get lost. The inter-crew honeymoon period soon ended. No matter as here, that the crew were all black. It made little difference. The hard slog of maintaining good relations lay ahead of them. It meant respecting one another's private space (what little there was), and continuing to do the job competently they were being paid to do.

Mandella was no trained psychologist like Sky. But in her experience of space tours, forced intimacy quickly became claustrophobic, however gregarious a personality you were. So she kept the crew busy. And kept herself distant from them. They didn't like her for it. She didn't expect them to — yet. One day, perhaps, when they ended the tour safe, intact and still sane, then they would thank her. Until then, she had to lead. Had to use her judgment to make difficult decisions and stick to them. And right now, she'd decided they needed drill. There was a casualness creeping in. It had started like that on her last ship...

Three shifts further into their journey to Thuli, while Kaya and Sky had been schlepping away their free time, Triple came across it — wildsurfed into a rogue signal. It didn't look like much. Pirate signals wilded about the Cosmos like so much dust, carrying news that was breaking, sometimes light years away. The transmissions were uncensored and often illegal. Listening was illegal too for zsf crews — such action did not have the approval of Command Control. Nor, for fear of overload or contamination, were wild signals processed by the ForceCode. For all that, Wilds were mostly harmless stuff. New pop songs, chat show gossip, fashion. As they came through in a scrambled combination of UV, radio and X-ray wavelengths, it took a gifted surfer to ride with one signal's woof and warp long enough to be able to lock onto the message. But, like riding an Urth ocean wave, Wilds surfing was a skill that was perfectible. And doing it gave a powerful buzz to the gifted practitioner. Right now

Triple was cresting:

"Yakka-roo!"

"Keep it down," issued Mandella sternly from her dais.

"Sorry, Captain," Triple said. He sneaked a look at the Captain. She had chosen to ignore his wilding. It was the first time he'd known her bend a rule.

"What's breaking, *binamadu*?" It was Sky, reappearing with a smile on the Bridge.

"Catch a hold of this!" Triple whispered.

Sky came and stood by his shoulder.

"A megatransmission from Kayiga. It's fierce locking on," Triple said working the console controls. The transmission was ultra faint. Sky watched Triple's screen as the autotranslators kept winking on and off. "Here, got it — take this," Triple said, handing over the controls, "I'm going to yank Kaya over. Kayiga's his folks' planet. Looks like they're having one big party there!"

Sky lunged to grab the controls as Triple jumped out of his seat. The young Surfer stayed long enough to correct the spin. "Just hold it there!" he grinned to Sky then dashed off.

Sky held on. Mandella looked at her disapprovingly.

"Let him have his fun," Sky soothed.

Mandella looked away. She'd indulged the youth already, allowing him to listen in to illegals. Now he was getting all the crew involved. That was what happened when you indulged people.

Triple cornered a reluctant Kaya in the corridor outside the Relax room

"You got to see this — it's Urthsome! I picked up Kayiga!" Triple waxed.

"It a move?" Kaya quizzed.

The irony bypassed Triple.

"No, no-no-no! It's right there where it was. But I'm picking up something giga. Like a biosphere bop party, or a miracle crop celebration. Sky's with it now."

"Cool," Kaya murmured. Triple took him by the sleeve and tugged him forwards. Kaya put his hand on the youth's shoulder to steady and slow him. Yet he couldn't deny that his heart leapt slightly. Any news from Kayiga would be a good feeling.

They made the Bridge and Kaya saw Mandella was there at her dais. She had her back to them and head down.

The rootsman and the youth crossed over to Lieutenant Sky at Triple's console.

"Any luck with the surf?" Triple buzzed, then to Kaya. "Look, can you make this out?" The screen was full of incoherent, scrolling code.

"Quiet," intoned Sky.

Both of them hushed in surprise.

"Is there a problem?" asked Triple finally.

"Yes and no," replied Sky.

Now Kaya was curious. "Doan riddle us, Lieutenant. What have you scanned?"

Sky turned and looked up calmly at the two of them. Their faces contrasted. Triple's boyish face was still glowing with excitement at his discovery. Kaya wore a more worried look. Right then, standing by her, he seemed all of his forty eight years. He had obviously grasped from the Lieutenant's manner that something was amiss.

"I'm sorry, Kaya…"

"A wha gwan?"

"Will somebody tell me? What have I happed on?" asked Triple.

Sky looked at Kaya, solemnly.

"You can tell me," Kaya nodded.

"Do you want somewhere private?"

"No. Just tell me."

"Sit down."

Kaya grabbed a chair. His mood now was a mixture of annoyance and dread.

"Tell me!" he said bluntly to her.

"What you're seeing is a massive execute-once data transmission."

"So?"

"All the knowledge ever acquired on Planet Kayiga is currently being transmitted in these bursts. That's why it's

13

flowing so fast."

Kaya looked away, distraught.

"I never seen data avalanche like this!" gleamed Triple. "And from so far. Why?"

The question was directed at Kaya.

Sky heard him. She could see Kaya was lost in thoughts, so she explained to the youth herself.

"It's a doomsday transmission," she said softly.

"Never!" said Triple proudly. "You mean, I, Officer Triple, I picked up a dooms—" Only now was it sinking in. *Doomsday transmission*. It meant Planet Kayiga was on the verge of some catastrophe.

"But what…?" started Triple.

"I don't know," said Sky,

"Maybe Omm can check the sensors," said Triple.

I'll ask the Captain presently." At this moment Sky was much more concerned with Kaya. "How feel you Kaya?" Kaya didn't answer. He looked becalmed. Lieutenant Sky sympathised. She knew what Planet Kayiga meant to Kaya. His parents were stationed on Planet Kayiga. He'd been birthed and raised by them there. Now, it seemed his parents and their environment were about to be destroyed forever…

Kaya got up and went unspeaking to his seat. His mind was giddy with questions: *What catastrophe? Why Kayiga? Why had he not been told?*

Captain Mandella saw Lieutenant Sky making her way over. The Captain knew what Sky would be asking, and had already decided that the answer was no. She wasn't being cruel. Once they had finished the job at Planet Thuli she would offer Officer Kaya three days standown on compassionate grounds. But not before. The ForceCode would back her on that. This was a Zimbabwe Space Force ship, not a love commune. They all had their professional duties to carry out.

"Captain—"

"Not now, lieutenant."

"Captain, you need to hear this."

"Does it relate to the Thuli mission?"

"No, Captain."

"Then I don't."

"You must be made aware. We have a personal trauma situation here. The ForceCode forbids you to ignore it."

Mandella eyed the lieutenant.

"There's nothing we can do. Nothing any of us in the space force can do."

"Do you know the cause of Kayiga's misfortune?" Sky pressed. Mandella had access to Command briefings. There was bound to be something mentioned on Kayiga.

Captain Mandella relented, touched the widescreen monitor on her dais.

"They sent me a background summary. Here, take a look."

Sky put a restraining hand on Mandella's.

"It's not me you need show this to, Captain, it's Officer Kaya."

Mandella winced. She had hoped to break it later. She was annoyed at Triple for having trapped the transmission, and at herself for having let him Wild. Her own slackness had got her into this.

"If you recommend," she replied reluctantly to Sky.

"I do," said Sky.

"All right. Go back to your station," she frowned.

Sky left Mandella and walked slowly up to Kaya. She gave him a brief shoulder hug and whispered something, then found her chair. Triple had wandered back to his own station on the Bridge.

Up on the dais Mandella felt nervous for a moment . She resolved to get it over with as quickly as possible.

"Officer Triple," the Captain's voice went into the flat, authoritative Captainspeak she used for giving orders: "we all know you've found something. How, I won't go into at this moment, but it will be logged. I'd like to be able to say what you found was quarknoise in the system. But the doomsday broadcast from Kayiga is the real thing." Mandella was watching faces, especially Kaya's. And she could see he wasn't taking it well. She continued nonetheless: "Command Control did not global this news because all interventions would be futile. That much is obvious from the data..."

Officer Kaya wasn't listening. He was thinking of his mother, who had heaved him into this world from between her own legs. Mama, who had let him suck the cream from her own breasts for two whole years, who had watched his first step, recorded his first cry, mentored his first thesis. And Papa... Papa who had always celebrated his kindergarten triumphs with a balloon party — his first word, his first crawl, his first tooth, his first rocket, his first space walk. Papa, who had buried his terrapins and said the prayers, that time when the water overheated and they'd died, Papa who rocked him in his arms that day, rocked him till he slept. Mama, Papa. They couldn't die...

Mandella was saying,

"If it makes it any easier, I'll show you how it came about."

The huge bow window of the bridge grew dark, and in place of the dust cloud of stars of the approaching Meridian Two, a chart of the Xanga Galaxy's Western hemisphere appeared. Mandella's commentary was sparse.

"You'll recognise Xanga Galaxy. The comet, Siva, measuring three hundred kilometres across, made its last appearance in Xanga two hundred million years ago. It was expected to pass by Xanga's sun with the minimum of disruption. Instead it entered the known Cosmos on a wildly eccentric orbit, and with a host of asteroidal comets in its wake"

"Why wasn't I told?" venomed Kaya.

"Because what difference could we make?" Mandella said tersely. She continued her explanation. "As Siva passed closest to the Xanga Galaxy's sun, it broke up. Thousands of comet fragments stormed through Xanga's solar system, destroying Kayiga entirely. Kayiga's defences have proved useless. They were not built to withstand an assault of such magnitude..."

Kaya was listening and not hearing. He was seeing things now. Making connections. And he resented Command's decision to keep him uninformed. And he resented Mandella's — as it must have been — brisk approval of their tactic. Now they'd been found out, they were telling him he was powerless in the face of the time-space gap between Kayiga and where they were now in Meridian Two. But was he? He doubted.

Mandella zoomed the charts: "The Xanga Galaxy is now in a state of flux. Planets out of orbit. Moons colliding — some merging, some disintegrating. Kayiga Planet's corona is filled with debris. The planet itself optically invisible."

"It isn't!"

"It isn't what, Officer Kaya?" Mandella edged.

"You're telling us Kayiga has been destroyed by meteorites?"

"Not me. The data says."

"It's a lie. Kayiga has not yet been destroyed."

"The charts are accurate maths. In relative time it's already happened."

Kaya demurred slowly,

"Not so."

"Kaya, you must feel—" Sky started. She could see confrontation looming.

"Hush!" Kaya boomed. Sky was out of her depths. He spoke cold reason to Mandella. "If Siva is behaving eccentrically, it is by definition not predictable."

"It depends on which timescale you're examining this event from, Officer Kaya," Mandella responded. "In terms of its trajectory, Siva is behaving eccentrically. But we're a hundred percent certain of its path through Xanga in the next twenty four hours."

"Urth hours?" said Kaya, already calculating.

"Yes," said Mandella.

That's certain, Captain?" asked Lieutenant Sky.

"It's official. All craft are too far away to attempt rescue." Then she said bluntly what needed to be said. "All life forms in Xanga will expire."

"The end will be painless?" Sky soothed.

Mandella ignored Sky and her soap. She was watching Kaya. "Officer Kaya, any intervention into the Xanga zone is useless. With all the turbulence there, we may in fact be witnessing the death throes of an entire galaxy."

"Shit!" Triple exclaimed, "we had a hundred million years to spot it, and this Siva just creeps up? Is that what you're saying, Captain?

"The reason why Siva has deviated from its orbit is not fully known," Mandella replied evenly, "but we are absolutely sure it will destroy Kayiga."

"You're saying there's nothing we can do?" Triple pressed.

"More than that. We are prohibited from any intervention. That is Command Control's order."

"And you'll follow that?" said Kaya bitterly.

"Of course."

"She is bound by protocol" added Sky.

"There's people on Kayiga, a whole colony. Including my parents."

"We know," Sky began. "We—"

"But you don't know," Kaya spat. "You have never known parents. None of you. Only me! You tests know nothing! Nothing!"

Mandella was unyielding.

"Of course there are deep emotions involved here. But we cannot abandon science for emotion. The science is clear. There can be no intervention. That way lies annihilation. "

"The Captain speaks true," intoned Sky, "though we feel your pain. All of us."

"To raas!" Kaya cursed them. "Nobody but a true Kayigan can know it. Or feel it!" But he cooled.

"Shag me, I'm shimballed," said Triple. "Why Xanga? There were eighteen million galaxies out there, and Siva has to pop up in one of only ten that are populated. That's a million to one chance. More."

"Million to one things happen all the time." Sky answered.

"Including death?"

"Random extinction is as naturally occurring as planetary life," she said.

"Well it sucks," replied Triple.

Which seemed to sum up the crew's mood.

"So, what now?" said Kaya finally, looking up from his workstation, to his captain. His deep voice trembled slightly as he asked.

Mandella spoke calmly, accentuating the positives to emerge from the disaster. She knew to do this. She was a disaster expert after her last ship, she thought, in a flash of remembered bitterness.

"The doomsday transmissions will ensure all knowledge acquired from colonisation of Xanga Galaxy, including Planet Kayiga, is saved for the good of allkind." She looked at her rocket engineer sincerely. "Officer Kaya, your parents' work will not have been in vain. Command has already transmitted their thanks to the Kayiga pioneers. Which thanks have been graciously received. Your parents have already been immortalised as heroes by a monument on planet Urth. As soon as is convenient, there will be a thanksgiving ceremony observed by at least one top rank from Zimbabwe Space Force, and maybe flowers." She watched Kaya shaking his head slowly, and wasn't sure what he meant by the gesture. "In the meantime," she pressed on, "our instructions are unambiguous. We are to continue our day-to-day duties. That is how we can best honour the Kayigans. By doing those duties well." There was silence. "Any further questions?" she sounded. There were none. "All right, you may take a halfsands of Free."

Mandella watched all three crew troop out. She had known about Kayiga's doomsday transmission all along, of course. But Command Control and the ForceCode had ordered the withholding of the information from the crew. Rightly, in her opinion. Emotions were messy things. They got in the way of clearthink. And one look at his record said Officer Kaya was not one to put emotions to one side. Fortunately she had made him see reason. She would record in the official log that she had handled the matter with tact and firmness.

After her last ship, Command Control would be observing her closely. A little worm of thought stirred in her. It said perhaps the whole Kayiga scenario was in fact a set up by Command, including the doomsday transmissions. They could be ruthless in their testing. She didn't pursue the thought further. There was no point trying to second guess Command Control. Real or test, the Captain believed she'd made the right decision on Kayiga. They were still on course for Thuli. The precious schedules were intact. Command could not fault her.

"How do you feel now, Kaya?" Sky probed. They were in Relax, just the two of them. Sky was in the therapists' position, lying on a parallel couch to Kaya, holding his left hand in her right, conducting grief counselling.

"Bug low." Kaya muttered.

"Do you have hate emotions for Command Control?" Sky asked.

"Yes, of course. I'd like to lick dem all…"

"This is grief, Kaya, you understand? A natural emotion."

"It a hurt," he said simply.

She squeezed his hand. "I sense you, Kaya, I sense you."

"My mother. She birthed me. It is not like test-tubing. I remember the moment she pushed me out into this world."

"We test-tubers will never share the closeness you had with your parents."

"A mother yells when she gives birth. The baby cries. And the mother laughs with relief recognising her baby's cry. They are joined by a cord called an umbilical. A tube that sustains and nourishes. The tube is cut by the birthing doctor. But the baby always remembers the join. Never forgets their two lives began as one."

"The baby grows, becomes independent."

"I hate them."

"Your parents?"

"Command. They are po-faced, pissing cowards to raas!"

This was good, thought Sky. Externalising the anger. She lay quiet as Kaya raged.

"A man travels the Universe at the behest of Command . He gives them everything he has — all his energies, all his dreams, a long lease of his life, he gives them all he has. But yet they doan tell him when his parents are about to…

"To die," Sky completed for him. "I'm sure, when they thought you were ready, they would have let you know."

Kaya became livid. "What? Am I a fool? An idiot? A madman? Is my soul not worthy of the knowledge? What respect do they show me, to hide this significant moment? To bury it in timesand, and only unsand it when the high tide of synchronity has passed? When time is stale for grief? No, Kaya is not a chiphead, to be bussed information at some other's convenience. I am a human, natural born. And Kaya demands deference when matters concern his own family!"

"There is deference. There is respect," Sky said calmly.

"Then why to raas Command not tell me a wha gwan straight away?"

"Maybe they were wrong…" She'd said it. Admitted it. It was not the first time she had said something against Command Control. Still she regretted it instantly, knowing there might be repercussions when Command went through e5's black box recording. But she wanted to show she was with him in his pain. Emotionally, her words were correct, had effect. Kaya calmed, lay back on the deep comfort couch. "They were very close to you?" Sky said gently.

"They hugged me. They loved me. They would never abandon me. Nor me them."

"You communicated with them often in adulthood?"

Kaya sighed.

"Birthdays, anniversaries. That order of kind. I wish I'd contacted them more."

"They were very important to you?

"Yes."

"They were very loving parents?"

"Yes."

"And now they're dead."

"Yes, Now they're dead."

Sky paused, let those words sink in. This time he'd said it. Said the big D word, Dead. It meant he was well on the way to being reconciled to their loss. Her job was done.

She held his hand silently for a while, acknowledging his grief. Then let go. She rose smoothly from her couch.

"I will leave you now. Lie still, Kaya, and remember the good times with your parents. You can be proud of them, as I'm sure they were proud of you."

"You are kind, sister."

"I leave you now: *Ku-tunza*."

Lieutenant Sky left Relax not feeling so good. She moseyed around the ship, making sure the others were all right, and eventually went to her sleepchamber. That night she recorded the following details in her private log:

Notes From Sky's Private Log

I have been present at the flowering of the most beautiful natural emotions. Kaya's tears fell in the open of the counselling room with me. The tremor of his aura was extremely moving. Its hurt spikes rose as he contemplated his parents' death. His was clean anger. The poetry of his face — its evanescent clouds; sadness, bewilderment, pain, joy at childhood memories; it was sublime... His pulse races, the heart palpitates, the pores open. Adrenal flush comes to the eyes. He calls it filial love. It is a beautiful dysfunction... The medical prognosis must be healthy in the long term . But ease of mind will not return to him for some while. He is many cycles from natural forgetfulness. His condition is operable and alterable by medication. He has refused both. The Captain requests to override his refusal surreptitiously, but at this moment I do not consent. The dissolution of the parental bond has released great emotional energies in him. Being close to his aura, I felt a strange sensation. I felt warm, happy and sad with him. I have not encountered this phenomenon before.

23

In the relaxation room Kaya looked around to make sure Sky had gone. Then he got up, smiling sourly. He'd fooled her. It was against regulations to refuse grief counselling. Sky would file the transcript with Omm and Omm would check it against a standard grief profile. He'd pass. Omm was smart, but he was smarter. No, he had fed her the line, but he, Kaya was far from resigned to his parents' death. Why should he be? It was a blatant lie to say there was no way of reaching Kayiga. Contrary to Mandella's bluff, the science said it was possible. She forgot he knew the science better then she did. He was born into it. Xanga Galaxy was one light year from where their craft now flew. That was close. Any craft with anti-matter Ramjets could get there before Siva, on his calculations. If zsf-e5 had been equipped with Ramjets, all they'd have needed to do was unhitch the freight, max the engines, and they'd be there at light two plus, faster than twice the speed of light. But ramjets were wobble technology, leading edge and expensive. They were only fitted on an elite fleet of command control craft, for use in a galactic emergency. Command Control obviously did not see the imminent deaths on Kayiga as such an emergency.

Of course, lowly zsf-e5 didn't have Ramjets. But there was an option open even to the humble ship: the black hole, Dogon III.

The more Kaya thought about it, the more it seemed possible. He glanced about him. A plan was forming. He had to keep it quiet, would have to wipe it even from his dreams since Omm sometimes tried to invade those too.

Black holes were the gateways of the Cosmos. They allowed instantaneous travel from one region of the universe to the next. The problem was avoiding the heart: how not be sucked into the black hole's infinitely dense core by its huge gravitational pull. If a craft was pulled into that core, it was instant annihilation.

The only safe way through a black hole was via the Einstein bridge. Each hole had an invisible ring around its outer edge, where the gravitational pull was mysteriously weaker. Hit this ring dead centre and you successfully re-emerged in another galaxy — in the case of Dogon III, in case Xanga. To take advantage of it, zsf e5 would have to fly into the outer edge of the black hole at a speed close to four hundred million miles per hour — almost warp speed.

Could zsf's engines do it? Well, Captain Mandella had asked him to tune them up. He would tune them, then repoint them for Dogon. It was a risk. If they didn't get up to speed, they'd fall into the black hole's heart. But he couldn't just abandon his parents, the way the tests were happy to. Blood was an imperative higher than the ForceCode orders, more important than Command Control's edicts.

He would do it. But he would need help getting past Omm's beady-eyed sensors.

On leaving the Bridge, Triple wandered aimlessly along the corridors for a while, before entering the Pleasure Store. It was the best way he knew of relieving stress. He stayed in the cubicle for a full sixteen minutes. When he re-emerged, his blood was flushed with after-sex endomorphins and he felt relaxed. But he was still depressed.

He was wandering some corridor — he didn't know or care which — when Kaya appeared and blocked his way. The rootsman pulled him over.

"Whap'n Bones!" Triple said, trying to sound happy.

Kaya took Triple by the arm, brusquely.

"Walk here!"

"What for?" Triple protested. He was not in the mood.

"This rahtid Fifteen engine!"

"But I don't know nothing about engines!"

"Doan argue."

Triple had never seen Kaya so vexed. Kaya took him by the arm and steered him along to the far end of the corridor they were in, down a set of ladders then along a series of dark, below-deck corridors. The throb of the engine room grew louder. But instead of taking Triple into the engineroom first stage airlock, Kaya turned them into a side corridor. Then pulled up.

It was dark. Only the weak red emergency lights shone. Triple could see Kaya's face. He was smiling conspiratorially. Triple remembered the engineroom corridors were not yet covered by Omm monitors — the Unions were still holding out. It was uncomfortable in these damper tile-lined, steel-railed and tin-floored walkways, but private. Every engineering craft crew in the space force used the facility to hang out away from the computers prying sensors. Kaya let go of his arm.

"That hurt!"

"Sorry."

Triple rubbed the bruised arm.

"So. What's the big wave?"

"You must help your brother."

"Sure, man. Anything you say."

"Me wan steer e5 through Dogon III to Kayiga."

"ARE YOU CRAZY?"

"Shh!" Kaya clamped Triple's mouth with his huge right hand. Omm would be groping to tune in with its nearest sensors. The engine mechanic waited till the kid had calmed, before removing his hand and letting him speak again.

"Are you crazy?" Triple whispered. "You can't do that. It's mutiny."

"Trust me, youth. I can do it. You don't believe?"

"I believe you, man, I believe you. But it's against—"

"Yeah, the rules. Omm would try fe stop me."

"That's if Mandella didn't ice you for it first."

"Don't worry 'bout Mandella. It's Omm is my problem. I can jettison the freight, realign the rockets. But I need you to lazy Omm so it doan override the settings."

Triple laughed nervously. "You're serious aren't you?"

Kaya held his eyes with his own. "Are you with me? If you can't do it, just say. I'll figure it myself."

"Ah," Triple squirmed, "don't give me that loyalty shit."

"C'mon kid. Yes or no?"

"But Dogon III," Triple stalled, "remember the Lamdart 16 singularity disaster?"

"Don't give me that!"

"They think there's a quantum blip in the aperture sizing. Lamdart was dusted…"

"I read the reports."

"Well?"

"Well what?"

"What's to say we won't hit the same blip? We'd be zeroed."

"You know what happened with Lamdart? I'll tell you. Lamdart 16 went in on the wrong trajectory. Command knows that. Their golden pilot focked up. They're just being cautious."

"I'm young, Bones. There's things I want to do still."

"Have faith. You'll live to party again, youth. "

"I don't know…"

"Please. I'm begging, *kijana*."

"Don't do this to me, Kaya."

"I'll pay you."

"I don't need money. I need a life."

"Sky's with me."

"She is?" Triple was surprised.

"Solid behind."

Triple wavered.

"…But what about my career?"

"I'll take the blame. Say I threatened you."

"What with?"

"With violence."

"They won't believe it."

"Why not?"

Kaya had his fist raised pressed against Triple's lips. The fist tasted tasted of petroleum oil. It was a bitter taste. Triple felt his upper lip being pierced by the edge of his own front teeth.

"But what makes you so sure you'll get it right where Lamdart failed?" Triple mumbled through the flesh of his pressed lips.

Kaya withdrew the fist, smiled again.

"Because I'm the best."

Triple thought.

"Ah, *fulani*," he said finally, "what a bummer!"

"Is that yes?"

Triple nodded mutely.

"*Asante, kijana!*" Kaya kissed him on the forehead.

Triple smiled weakly.

"When can you do it?" quizzed Kaya.

"Give me time," Triple said.

"Now?"

"Right now?"

Kaya smiled. "Thank you, brudda. Much respect."

"Yeah." Triple pulled himself free of Kaya's embrace and headed back through the corridors to the bridge. How could he have said no? And yet, how could he have said yes? It was not the task itself. Bypassing Omm was easy. Behind its arrogant facade, Omm was a hodgepodge of blustering code. You simply tied it up with a Van-Rimmer equation, then dived into that soft underbelly. From there, you disabled the alarm cpu's. Their shadow then resurfaced, with Omm none the wiser and still battling it out with the Van-Rimmer. He'd done it three times already out of boredom. No, Omm was not the problem. It was Captain Mandella.

When the Captain found out she'd be furious. And she would find out. If he wasn't caught in the act, it would become obvious as soon as the freight was jettisoned. If they survived the black hole, and the Siva asteroids, they'd have to face the music with Mandella. She was a control freak, bound to come down heavy on them. It would be years on ice, minimum. He was crazy to do this. The whole idea was crazy. Dangerous crazy. The only thing to do was to call it off. But then he couldn't face Kaya. The way Kaya was, he might not live that long if he refused to help. It was a double neg. scenario.

The moment Captain Mandella noticed something was wrong was when one of her dais alert panel icons winked. She didn't know its significance immediately, not ever having seen that particular icon active before, and she had to touch down the Quiz box. By the time she had done so, Omm had intervened. The wink had become a constant glow, and a Second Amber alert klaxon was sounding throughout the craft.

The crew reconvened on the Bridge. This time they didn't grumble. Second Amber was too serious. Mandella wised them from her dais:

"the hulk appears to have self-jettisoned."

"Are you sure?" asked Lieutenant Sky, puzzled. "We would have felt something — a jolt."

"Check the clock," Mandella said coldly. It was what she had already done.

Dutifully, Lieutenant Sky checked the atomic clock. Sure enough, time in the craft was running six billionths of a second slower. It meant their craft had picked up speed. Sky touched down the speedo which confirmed this. They were travelling at two hundred million mph, and accelerating. No way could they do such speed with the hulk in tow.

"You're right, we've lost the hulk," were the only words that Sky managed.

They were also drastically out of orbit, Mandella knew. "Officer Kaya, reverse engines!"

It was as if he hadn't heard her.

"Officer Kaya!"

"No can do," Officer Kaya said.

"Dogon is on the horizon," Mandella began, not registering the smirk on Kaya's face. "This is an emergency, Officer Kaya. Apply max reverse thrust now!"

Officer Kaya did not act.

Mandella weighed it. Maybe he'd frozen. People reacted differently under pressure. You never knew until a genuine emergency just how any individual would react. Mandella turned to her Gunner.

"Officer Triple — take over engine control! Hurl us round!"

Officer Triple took up engine-control. He optioned reverse thrust. As he expected, nothing happened. He himself had switched off Omm's rocket control processors. He looked to Mandella and shrugged.

"What's going on?" Mandella said. She looked at the monitors, puzzled. Then back at Kaya. He was still frozen. Then Triple. The Gunner avoided her eyes. She could see now, some conspiracy was underway. Either Officers Kaya and Triple must have jettisoned the hulk and locked the engines. She checked the course. Dogon III. It all clicked. Kaya. His whole plan came to her. She turned abruptly. Looked through the bow membrane. Dogon III was already apparent. Imminent calamity. Desperately now, Captain Mandella interrogated the ForceCode to see what it could do. But it fuzzed her. Fuzzed her when she needed it most. What damn use was the damn ForceCode if it couldn't deal with a crisis?

She calmed herself. There had to be a solution. She started on the flash diagnostic routines. She had sixty-six zsf seconds to reverse the rockets, then they'd be too close to Dogon and it would all be over.

As Mandella hacked away at Omm, Officer Kaya spoke languidly.

"Doan bother, Captain. The rockets are on mechanical auto. Out of reach of Omm."

"And how do you know that?" she snapped.

"I put them there."

So she was right. There was always one. No matter how carefully you select,-and Mandella hadn't had the choice this time round, the crew was imposed — there was always one you had to look out for. The dangerous one. On zsf e5, that one was Officer Kaya. *I put them there.* he'd said. She didn't believe him. She turned to Triple. "Officer Triple. Switch the Code back on. Fast."

"Yes, Captain."

Again she'd guessed right.

Kaya shot Triple a threatening glance.

Triple looked to his Captain. Then to Kaya. Kaya shook his head for him to refuse.

Triple froze. He couldn't please them both.

"Triple! Have you taken leave of your senses? Fifty-three seconds! This course is suicidal."

Still Triple dithered.

Captain Mandella swore. "Fuck!" Then she turned to Sky and pleaded.

"Lieutenant Sky!"

Sky tried.

"Kaya, you have set us on course for Kayiga, via Dogon III. Is that true?" she asked calmly.

"That's right." Kaya didn't mind telling her, or Mandella, now.

"Perhaps you could reassure us of the flight path through Dogon III." Sky hoped to encourage reasoned debate on the safety of his action. Though she knew a decision guided by emotion was rarely changed by reason. All the while she was thinking how she'd misread him, how he'd fooled her in grief counselling.

"The path's safe," Kaya insisted, "We'll crash through the outer event horizon at Dogon's equator. Density there is not critical due to the Schwarzschild rotation effect. The vertical aperture is six hundred and fifty metres. We'll be past the outer and then the inner event horizon, head along the Einstein bridge, emerging in Xanga."

Twenty two seconds. Mandella heard Kaya so calm, and she cursed under her breath. The sheer stupidity of his action was beyond words. Schwarzschild had not got his maths right on Dogon. Two lost craft were testament to that. Now Kaya was intent on zsf becoming the third.

"Perhaps it is safe," replied Sky to Kaya, calmness personified, "but since this is not certain, maybe we, the other crew whose lives are involved here, perhaps we should have a say too?"

"Doan matter now," Kaya said, "we're entering Dogon's

gravitational field. "

Lieutenant Sky turned to Triple.

"Triple," she asked him. "are you sure this is the right thing?"

"Well, I'm not sure, but—"

"Do you feel you have done right by us all?"

"He begged me — he said you were with him as well. "

Sky went cold.

"That's not true. I would never have approved such a rash deed."

Triple's face fell and Sky saw he too had been duped by Kaya. "Triple," she pleaded, "is there nothing you can do?"

"We're almost there," Kaya cut in.

"Turn us back, Triple." Sky held Triple's eyes with hers, pleading.

Triple looked down and away.

"It's too late," he mumbled.

Mandella intervened.

"So, we get through the black hole. Into Xanga. What about Siva?" she asked Kaya acidly.

Kaya was irritated by the question. The answer was obvious in the maths. "Siva won't have arrived there yet. We'll be four hundred thousand miles ahead of Siva. And that's using Command Control's own data."

"That's no time at all," Mandella said, exasperated, "a scintilla, the nose of a gnat." She was standing at her dais, clutching the motion rail.

"That's where we're gonna fly then," Kaya smiled right back at her, "right up the nose of a gnat!"

There was no point now in arguing, they all knew. The readings showed the gravitational field about them was now so strong, they were irreversibly locked into Dogon III.

As the force got heavier, the ship's membranes blacked out, as did the lighting. Mandella shut down all but the core systems to protect against surges.

The velocity readings rolled up to four hundred and sixty four million kph. The crew felt their bodies slowing, becoming immense. The ship's sensors showed they were aligned about the collapsed star's disc-shaped equator. There was no sound on board, apart from the distant hum of the engines. The velocity counter edged forward another fraction.

"V-counter at critical. It's going to flip now," murmured Kaya.

And it did. Mandella sensed the ship tilt into the Dogon III aperture. It took an instant. Would it take their lives?

Mandella stirred. The ship's secondary systems had begun powering up automatically, and the lights were back on full. She saw Kaya. He was suppressing a bitter know-it-all smile as he scrolled navigation charts. Mandella looked to her own console. They were in Xanga Universe. Kayiga was South South West. That much was fine and cause, if must be, for smirking. But where was Siva? She couldn't tell. There was not enough geostatic data. What she had to do, wherever Siva might be, was get the ForceCode rockets control back on-line, then steer them out, hyperfast.

She left her dais, and walked over to Triple. He was still slumbering. She shook him. He grunted himself awake. Mandella was over him, her face a grim mask.

"Huh?" Triple didn't really know what was going on.

"Get the engine cpu's active. I want control of the engines back."

Kaya was awake and alert to her.

"After I've picked up my parents, I'll give you back control," he breezed.

"No! I am the captain of this ship. Officer Triple, connect the code now!" Mandella seethed.

Triple rose and made to move to the surf console where he could ride the code best.

Kaya stood blocking his way.

"Don't do it, Triple."

Triple's big feet stopped.

"Get a move on. It's an order," said his captain behind him.

Triple stepped forward.

Then Kaya hit him — punched him low in his stomach. Triple doubled up, more surprised than hurt. He felt another blow to the back of his head. That was all.

"Anyone else?" Kaya stared defiantly. He was face to face with Mandella.

Mandella made a mental note. If she lived through this, she was damn well getting an all-female crew next time.

Then the ship shifted. It lurched to starboard. Mandella grabbed for a hold. Any hold. Didn't make it. She spilled onto the deck. The ship straightened. Then lurched again, this time to port.

It was the waves. Mentally Mandella kicked herself. She should have known She hauled herself up. Kaya was still down. She made no attempt to close on him. She was thinking. The slight bumps they had been experiencing since entering Xanga Galaxy. She had thought they were mere space curves. But they had been growing in size. Space curves didn't do that. It must be Siva, on their tail and closing.

"That's Siva," she accused Kaya. He'd got up now.

"It can't be," the engineer countered. But there was more shock than certainty in his voice.

The ship rocked again. An almost fifteen degree tilt.

"Let me ask the ForceCode," Mandella said. "-the geo-positioning sensors."

Kaya refused.

"Don't think to fool I."

"Let Triple surf then. See what he finds."

Kaya nodded assent. So long as Triple didn't reconnect Omm rockets control, their course would be as he, Kaya, had set.

Triple was coming round. Mandella helped him and the young Gunner got up. Mandella told him what to do. He made a wide berth round Kaya, sat at the surf console and set to it. His stomach still felt sore but he knew the seriousness of the situation. They were depending on him.

Lieutenant Sky was awake now. She watched them

silently; Mandella looking murderous, Kaya truculent, young Triple nervous and upset.

"There's a transmission on zsf emergency frequency. Command thinks we're lost. Do we respond?" Triple said

"Just focus on Siva, *fulani*" Mandella cursed him.

Triple surfed on.

Mandella ordered the rest of the crew back to their consoles, and to strap in to their seats. Kaya complied, as did Sky.

At the console, Triple racked his brains. His stomach was aching from that punch. The back of his neck was knotted with pain. Kaya had cracked. He didn't trust him any more. But Kaya still scared him. He had to find Siva. Mandella was relying on him.

It didn't take long. He brought Siva on screen — she was a giant vector force, gaining on them every second. There was no way they could outpace her. That much was instantly obvious. Wordlessly, Triple looked to Kaya.

Kaya met the youngster's gaze, resolutely.

"We can tek dem, spar — Siva will slow," he murmured.

Triple turned back to his console. Couldn't Kaya see? Didn't he feel the shock waves, getting bigger and bigger? What more could he show him? Their course was nonsensical. It was clear and distilled that they were dead. Through the static, he found a zsf-coded Kayiga radio transmission. He snapped it straight through. It came garbled and squawking.

"What's that?" Mandella muttered.

"Shh," said Triple.

He cleaned it so it came through clear:

"This is the Elder BabaKayatunde of Planet Kayiga: Turn back SonKaya. You should not have come…"

Kaya sat transfixed. It was the voice of his father.

"SonKaya, hear this. Your craft is being caught by Siva. Turn away from Kayiga. You have no right to endanger your compatriots. Uphold the honourable reputation of our family. The glory of Kayiga was in its high principles. Sacrifice. Dedication. Resistance against oppression. Generosity of Spirit. Kayiga had a proud history. Its destiny shall continue with you and all Kayigans of the multiversal Diaspora. Remember this. That is how you will honour us. Now turn away before it is too late."

Kaya's left hand smeared the moisture on his cheek.

"Kaya?" called out the Captain, "Is that enough? Kaya!"

Kaya sat there.

"Shock, Captain," Lieutenant Sky surmised.

Mandella moved smartly. "Officer Triple, trip the cpu's back now."

"But—"

"Don't babble. Do it."

A huge shock wave hit them. rolling them ninety degrees. Siva was here now, its foreshocks so immense they were about to be swallowed. Triple surfed for his life. He primed the Van-Rimmer. Ducked into the raw code. Re-enabled Omm's engine control processors. It took him three seconds flat. He came screeching out of the code, and nodded to Mandella: "All yours, Captain."

Mandella looked down at her dais. The rocket control icons were winking again. Kaya was still zombied, but she knew enough. In a flurry of code executions she span zsf out of its apocalyptic trajectory, and steered hard. For Dogon Two...

Zsf-e5 corkscrewed up. Siva rushed on. Its left vortex threatening to swipe them.

Mandella kept to the steep climb.

They could hear the engine crying out in pain.

The craft shook at its welds.

Siva charged. The biggest wave ever hit. They were clipped. It flung the craft into a tailspin.

Mandella clung on, unravelled them. Hauled them up again. Burst the engines on maxthrust, gimbal on auto. Even Triple admired the move. In a whine of mechanical exhaustion, zsf screamed out of Siva's path.

Slowly, they pulled further away into calm black void. Captain Mandella piloted zsf through the Dogon II's gateway out of Xanga and back into Meridian Two.

As was her duty, Captain Mandella contacted Command Control to report. She told them they had entered Xanga via Dogon III to reconnoitre Planet Kayiga. They had left immediately they saw the situation irrecoverable. There was no immediate response from Command.

Calmly, the Captain waited. If she lost this ship, she'd lost it faster than the first. Maybe they'd retire her. Put her on sick leave. She didn't care. For sure she'd had enough of this crew. Three months, and she'd already had her fill of them.

Command finally got back to her. Pettifogging.

"Would she repeat her transmission please?" The voice of a Command clone.

She repeated it. There was another delay. They were probably checking the retirement dome lists for vacancies, and calculating what her payoff entitlement would be if they released her, and whether they could dismiss her without Union litigation. She didn't give a row of beans. She sat calmly.

When the official response came, Mandella couldn't believe her screen:

Command praises Captain Mandella's pioneering spirit and calculated bravery. In using the black hole Dogon III, zsf-e5 has re-established beyond dispute its navigability. Zsf-e5 has led the way where other crews must follow. The military and economic benefits of re-establishing the Dogon III route are significant. Hail the Captain. Hail the crew. There will be a ceremony on Urth, including a plaque to be erected on the wall of a civic Urth building, subject to confirmation.

Mandella protested. Switching to analogue, the Command clerk cut her short. Command's higher echelons did not care to know about "dissent" on board e5. And it was not proper to use the word "mutiny". Her nomenclature protocols were not in order. They would be expunged from the data. Captain Mandella was an official hero. It was a duty. She was to bask in the glory. Mandella signed off. She wastebinned the resignation speech she had prepared to deliver to the crew and turned to face them.

She'd forgotten to raise the level bars and the crew had been privy to it all.

"Ride the vibe, Captain," Triple jested.

Kaya said nothing.

Sky looked to Mandella puzzled. Command was never usually lenient. They were scheming something.

Mandella shrugged. She was inclined to adopt Triple's view. After the shame of her last ship, she liked being hot property with Command again; but you could never fully trust them to stick with a deal, and she had this niggling feeling that, in the long run, it would rebound badly. There again, she had that feeling about anything good that happened to her. Lieutenant Sky had called her a bonesure pessimist.

Notes From Sky's private log

This feeling washes over me of emotional exhaustion. Space is a frightening, isolating environment, artificial in the extreme. Technology — rocketry, telemetry etc — has advanced faster than human beings have evolved. There is a stark gap between the human and the artificial that soft implants and genesplicing can only do so much to bridge. Bewilderment, rage, neuroticism and paranoia are all very human reactions to long-term exposure to the space environment. My role as healer is to lay myself down, act as a bridge between the soft and the organic.

Kaya's psychic wounds are especially deep. He has this

astonishing power of emotions. His parents' death has upset him. He has shown physical symptoms of distress: soreness of the eyes, hoarseness of the throat, migraine, heaviness of the limbs. He is withdrawn, irritable and has a shortened attention span. I have offered him Dopalax, but he refuses to take it. He tells me he is "born to suffer". I diagnose incipient clinical depression. It shows in his severely distressed aura. My task is to settle, to calm, to heal. How far I can do that with Officer Kaya I do not know. I have problems connecting with him. His violence over Kayiga, the way he betrayed Triple's trust and deceived us both, suggests he is a powerful dissembler. I realise now how little I really know him.

Perhaps, ultimately, we are all alone, in our own worlds, merely orbiting each other. Maybe Captain Mandella's advice was correct and I should have sedated Kaya against his will, immediately after the doomsday transmission.

Triple is very subdued. He avoids eye contact with everyone. My last physical on him revealed random, infrequent heart palpitations. His hands tremble. There is a significant drop in testosterone level. He is finding it hard to relate to the others again in the way that he used to. Perhaps he never will relate in his old way. Kaya has changed completely in his eyes, I sense. Before he was an idol. Now he has become fallible, as all idols must. Triple is wrestling to reconcile his former images of Officer Kaya with the hard truth of his human flawedness. Also I think Officer Triple has understood that the incident showed he himself has flaws. He was too easily led by Kaya. This has upset his confidence. He has low self-worth.

Overheard:

TRIPLE: Kaya?
KAYA: Scram!
TRIPLE: Kaya!

KAYA: You heard me. Slime!

I have seen Triple slumped in the relaxation room, sucking his thumb. He mutters in his sleep. The contrast with his ebullient self is stark. I comfort him with smiles, a reassuring word, my hand on his shoulder. He fears judgment of his conduct. I do not judge. The most huge sun is the coldest thing compared with human warmth. This is what he needs, what he lacks.

The Captain distrusts the crew even more now. She is more driven. Her eyebrows plunge, her pupils narrow when she is approached. She eats alone. Her self-isolation has reached a dangerous extreme. People need people on a level deeper than the functional. It is Mandella's duty, I will tell her, to herself and to the crew, to relax. She is scared to let go — to forgive herself. She has been hard-shocked by the Kayiga incident. Coming on top of her troubles with her last ship, I understand. She is traumatised. But she will exhaust her psyche if she does not ease up on herself soon.

Kaya sat at his console, his face a mask of indifference. He'd watched the Captain lapping up Command's praises for reopening Dogon III. Yet it was he, Kaya, who had reopened Dogon III. And if Mandella hadn't held out so long they could have saved his parents, whatever his father said.

Kaya gouged his psychic wound. Why had Mandella frustrated him? Had she wanted his parents dead? She'd put her precious schedules before their lives. What kind of person could do that?

He looked at her. *The so-called captain. She stands there at the dais. Never tires. Never shows any emotion. Listens to no music. Never laughs. Never even smiles. She is not human, not even humansoft. She is a Command Control clone. A robot.*

The thread of thought whirled and span in Kaya's head. *A robot. Clearly. Why else her unthinking adherence to the*

41

ForceCode, to Command Control commands? Why else does she never allow anyone close to her? In case we see the joins?

We are being led by a robot. It is another Command economy. Robots don't need paying. All this rumour stuff about she lost her last ship etcetera, it was all a cover story to explain her distance, her strict routine. The routine of a robot. She has no personality, no quirks, no little foibles or flaws, and she never recognises, never respects, never allows for them in others. Mandella can't deal with flaws because robots can't understand them.

Kaya could see it now. Could see something else too. She was reducing them to robots too. Turning the entire crew into efficient, low-cost, high conforming drones.

Of course the others were taken in. Triple was too scared of her to see it. No doubt Lieutenant Sky could work up some human-consistent psychological explanation for the Captain's behaviour — the lieutenant was never short of a theory. Only he, SonKaya, was wise to her. Or, more correctly, to it. And he was going to do something about it. He swore revenge on the robot. The very idea reanimated him.

"Kaya?"

"Yes, youth?" Kaya's face was lit up.

"Hey, so you're back?"

"I never been gone, kid."

"Kumbe!" cried Triple

"What's eating you then?"

"I'm bored. Wanna splurgechase next freetime?"

"Prepare to be whupped!"

"Go deh, bones! Listen, I've been meaning to say, if I did anything wrong, then—"

"Don't say anything."

"With Kayiga and all that—"

"Nothing."

"Eh?"

Kaya looked at Triple's confused, earnest face and smiled at him. A large, disarming smile. "I doan wanna hear you 'pologising, youth. The blame doan lie with you."

Triple's face clouded a moment, but he dismissed the

thought, happy to be hearing from the old Kaya again —
surely this was the old Kaya?

"Awooah!" he yelled. "The FunRoom then, next Free?"

"I'll be there, kid," grinned Kaya.

"Officer Triple — back to your station!"

"Ah, shit," Triple said to Kaya under his breath. "Captain again."

"Mandella's not shit — shit's organic," Kaya said.

"Huh?"

Kaya didn't explain.

"Dig up back to your base before she mouths off at you again,"

Triple slouched away. What was that about organic Kaya had said? Triple wasn't sure Kaya was the full manual yet, but he was happy he speaking with him again.

"Permission to approach the dais, Captain?" called out Sky.

"Permission granted."

Lieutenant Sky approached.

"How long do you intend to keep this up?" she whispered.

"What, lieutenant?" Mandella replied softly.

"Drills. Exercises. Routines. Constant cold looks. A team needs encouragement if it's to play well together."

Mandella's voice picked up ice.

"They're not here to play. They're here to work. They've played around too much already."

"You're angry still. It's understandable. But why not deal with your anger? Face them. Allow them to understand how you feel. Punishing them like this, you punish yourself. Constant negativity crushes the spirit."

"Then spirits can crush. I've seen it all before on my last ship. I was that close back there to losing ship number two, all crew included, me included."

"Are you sure you are not motivated by prejudice?"

"Me?"

"Yes. You are from Ghana sector. Ghana have had their disputes with the Kayigans."

"Don't trivialise my actions, Lieutenant. Don't you ever trivialise me, understand?"

"Very well, Captain."

Mandella calmed.

"Officer Kaya transgressed. Officer Triple aided and abetted. Only you have clean hands. It was a joint conspiracy. Now I'm going to crush them—"

"They're people, Captain, not cartons to be crushed. Officer Triple's very young. Captain, are you listening?"

"Yes."

"Don't give up on them."

"Is that all, lieutenant?" Mandella said.

"I worry for you."

"Is that all?" she repeated coldly.

"Yes, Captain."

"You may go," Mandella dismissed her. She watched Sky return to her station. No doubt Lieutenant Sky was sincere. But the lieutenant over-empathised with the two males. Saw them as merely misguided. Mandella could not see them in that benign light. What they had done repelled her. The thought still made her physically sick. Mutiny. No other word described it. She had to punish them. Drills in the first quarter. Exercises in the second and third. Then more exercises. A short sleeptime. Then reveille, and drills again. They were on the fourth day of the new regime. Mandella piloted the ship towards Thuli herself while the crew drilled. It was not just punishment. Things had gotten slack long before before the Kayiga Incident. Now, if anyone could see, they would say, 'Mandella runs a tight ship — there are no slackers in her crew'. It was the duty of the Captain to mould the crew's characters, their reflex behaviour, until they were "the right stuff". Only then could she relax, if then. Only then could she trust, and let them use their discretion. And the crew still had a long way to go. Command was never going to allow an all-black crew to be merely average. Average wasn't good enough. They had to be the best. Even if they were just an engineering ship, they had to be the best run engineering ship.

From the dais, the captain eyed Kaya. Of all the crew, he was the one she would ship out at the earliest opportunity. She detested him. She detested his hair. The locks were filthy. They symbolised a millennium-old outlook. She didn't like his nose — it was too squashed; or his eyes — too dilated; or his mouth, too loose. He didn't shower enough, so he smelt. He was prone to sulkiness and ill-discipline. He had already had a malign influence on Officer Triple, who spent too much time in his company. What Triple saw in him she did not know. A father figure she guessed. As far as she was concerned Kaya knew too much — knew every Union dodge going, and more besides. In the first three months he had constantly quoted Union rules to her, yet flagrantly broke the ForceCode's most sensible edicts when it suited him.

Now, with the new regime she had instituted after the Incident, Officer Kaya had changed. She was sure she was breaking him. He alternated long bouts of serenity with outbreaks of extremely bizarre behaviour. The latter included dropping things suddenly at her feet. Loud, tuneless whistling. Shining magnesium lights around the Bridge on the pretext of maintenance inspection. And carrying around small, weird, homemade electrical apparatus. She'd stamped hard on it of course, whenever such behaviour broke out. But she was privately pleased. She wanted him to break totally — for his psyche to smithereen. Then she would move for his summary dismissal on medical grounds. How Kaya had survived so long in the space force she didn't know. But it was time he was exposed. He had jeopardised her career, her crew, her ship.

She looked again from the dais and saw Sky massaging Officer Kaya's shoulders. Mandella pursed her lips in silent disapproval. Officer Kaya didn't need hand massage. He needed electric shock treatment.

★

Over the next shifts Captain Mandella continued to drive them. The orders came remorselessly from shift to shift and from day to day. She was punishing them. She wanted to hurt them. She hated them with all her might.

Of course the source of Mandella's hatred was fear. A fear so charged, so dangerously unresolved for her, it would blow her conscious mind if ever she had to face it so it only surfaced raw and naked in the nightmare landscape of her sleep. It was a fear fuelled by charred memory:

The Hunter the Hunter, no, no, no, the Hunter!
   -MISSILES OFF! MISSILES OFF!
   -VIS-ID NOT CONFIRMED AT 4-4 CAPTAIN! 3-4 ONLY!
   -OVERRIDE! MISSILES OFF! (DNNNNK) WE ARE TARGET
   LOCKED! AT DEEP SPACE SEVEN!
   -ESCAPE VECTOR IMPOSSIBLE!
   -EJECT! EJECT!
   (BBHWOOOOSH!)

★

On Day Circadian 128: Shift Four Expired, the three crew were scheduled to be in deepsleep. But, though Lieutenant Sky and Officer Triple lay inert on their sleepchamber berths, the prone form of Officer Kaya stirred. He raised himself up. He had thought about this for a long time. Not the whether, more the how. It was not murder. You do not murder a robot. You decommission it. He was going to section its head with a plastic, high tensile bladed saw. Why the head? He realised there was no solid engineering reason for a robot to have its main control centre in the head region. It was merely a hunch.

Kaya folded back his blanket and pulled on his tunic. He eased his quarters wardrobe door back and took out the pillow and the heavy hack he'd hidden there. Then he stole over to the crew sleepchamber door. One glance back told him the others were still deeped. He held down the chamber door access button gently so it didn't click.

Then he was out.

He padded his way along the corridor from the dorm to the bridge, hacksaw in one hand, pillow to trap the fluidsin the other. He guessed Mandella would still be on the bridge at her dais. The Captain never stood down. It had puzzled him when he'd first noticed this — how indefatigable she was. But it was obvious now. Since she was a robot she needed no sleep. It was so obvious the others hadn't thought of it. Yes, she would be on the Bridge. The corridor lights had dimmed, as always at Shift Four Expired. As Kaya walked, his long shadow chased ahead of him. He recalled his strategy. He would approach from the rear, bring the hack down like an axe. It should cut through the epidermal shell. There would be spurts of fluid. He'd stop them splattering with the pillow. When the fluids had drained, he'd hack through the wires. He estimated a maximum twenty two kilowatts of power in an android of that size. Easily enough to fry him. Which accounted for the plastic blade of the heavy hack.

Kaya had already tested the vision and hearing range of the Captain-machine. While greater than that of the average human, it was still within the general human range. It did not detect movement to the rear. Nor uhf sounds. At first it puzzled him. They could have given it greater powers. But then he figured it. Command had guile. They knew that if the android's powers were too exaggerated, the crew would notice. They had fooled his colleagues, Kaya thought, as he padded stealthily along the corridors. But not SonKaya. As an expert in Organics, from a family of experts, he was the hardest of all to fool. That was why the robot scapegoated him, kept its distance from him.

Still, somewhere in the back of his mind came the whisper: *But*.

The Captain machine kept its humourless distance from them all. Because feelings, emotions, were the most complex and subtle of human attributes, they were impossible to fake for long. Interacting with the crew off-duty, the robot would have been found out, laughing in the wrong places, smiling when there should be a grimace on its face, talking when silence was the appropriate response. Kaya saw the programmers' dilemma, almost sympathised with them. Their solution had been to limit its emotional range simply to sternness and aloofness. It had worked for a while. But once you saw through it, you saw how inadequate a solution it was. And he, Kaya, had seen through it. Now he was going to expose Command's deceit for them all to see.

But, but. What if it was not a robot? What if it was human or humansoft, like the rest? Kaya's doubting voice was faint. The noise of his rational self drowned it out. All the facts fitted his conclusion. He was certain they were dealing with a robot.

As Kaya closed the sleepchamber door behind him, another person in there stirred. Lieutenant Sky. She'd heard Kaya rising. Now something told her to follow him. She thought at first he was sleepwalking, but the furtive way in which he dressed, gathered objects from his robe, then stole away, said that that was not the case. And he had a worrying air of purpose about him. Sky dressed quickly. Her intuition was hurtling to a series of malign conclusions. She unlocked her safe and took down her stunner. She wouldn't use it unless absolutely necessary.

In the eerie half light of Shift Four Expired, the ship hummed softly. Most of the internal sensors were stood down to conserve energy. It became possible to like the ship, in this soft light. Kaya felt the spongy vanilla-tiled walls of the corridor. They were semi-organic, impregnated with a host of microbes which fed off carbon dioxide and gave back oxygen. These walls were normally the ship's main supply of oxygen. They had voyaged thousands times thousands of miles, sustained by this basic microbic gaseous exchange.

Kaya reached the Bridge doors. He activated the airlock as quietly as he could. If the Captain-Machine questioned him, he planned to say he was refreshed and wanting more practise on the rocket control simulators for the tricky Thuli docking procedure ahead. That would confuse it. It accorded with Best Practice Protocol. The robot could hardly refuse.

He made inside the Bridge. He didn't see the Captain-Machine at the dais. Puzzled, his eyes swept round.

Finally, he spotted it. It was at the dais, to the far end, positioned in an unusual sitting posture in a chair, head framed by the left arm. The other arm hung loose. It appeared to be at rest. Dormant. Recharging perhaps.

Kaya approached stealthily.

Sky had watched Kaya's steady mental deterioration in the days following the Kayiga misfortunes with mounting trepidation. She asked herself now, Was he now in hyperpsyche? Had the trauma of loss been not resolved by sleep and time as was text, but rather fermented and distorted by Captain Mandella's punishing drill schedules and her wilful refusal to pro-communicate? Had mad hallucination now displaced common sense in the rocket engineer's fevered mind? It was not unknown. Lieutenant Sky had sensed he was cracking, had noticed the little things and had done her best to get him through.

Now she watched him slink along the corridor, followed him from a distance. She saw a pillow under one arm, and a bulky object in the clenched hand of the other. She watched him as he passworded through the airlock doors and entered the Bridge.

She could not see him when he passed onto the Bridge. Not clearly. But she guessed Mandella. *Kaya and Mandella.* A bad mix alone. She hurried. She didn't trust. And she found this not trusting a strange experience. She made it to the airlock doors, passworded them. The doors glided.

The lieutenant kept to the side.

She saw Kaya well forward on the Bridge, and heading for the dais. He didn't turn. Hadn't seemed to notice her. The Bridge doors slid back silently. She kept to the side, not moving. She saw Mandella in her chair on the dais, sleeping. She saw Kaya advance on the prone Mandella.

Kaya raised the object, his face a picture of concentration. Nervously, Sky felt for her stunner. She had never shot anyone before. But now the time was upon her, she didn't shrink from the responsibility.

★

Kaya stood over it. Its eyes were closed. It showed no sign that it had detected his presence. Its back rose and fell slightly in the rhythm of human lungs. It was a good simulacrum of a human being, he gave it that.

If he was to strike, he must do it now, quickly. He raised the heavy hack ready to sweep its blade down on the neck.

Sky's back was braced against the wall of the Bridge. She had the stunner raised and he was square in her sights. She knew it was her duty to shoot. It would not be lethal. But it would destroy Officer Kaya's career. It would finish him in the Force. She willed him not to do it: *Kaya — don't force me...*

The blade reached the peak of its upward arc...Then something caught Kaya's eye. Something peculiar about it. He had never seen it do that before. In the loose hand, between the fingers,was a black, crushed velvet swatch. A lucky charm from Urth. He looked up again at the face. The eyelid hinges worked. The nano-pneumatics of the face made light spasms. A globe of clear fluid rolled out from under the left eyelid. The nose sniffed. The hand supporting the head shuddered. Then sound came from the mouth, faintly: *"Reverse Thirteen! Reverse Thirteen! Thirteen now!"* A second globe of water followed the first from the same eyelid.

Kaya was thrown. Did robots dream? Did robots cry? His killing hand eased down. Without thinking, with his other hand, he eased the pillow under his captain's head.

Captain Mandella dreamed on.

Officer Kaya passed Lieutenant Sky at the doorway. Sleepwalked right past her. Sky stood there, frozen, as he passed. When he was gone, she felt her spirit soar. She let out an audible sigh.

Suddenly a voice rasped.

"What are you doing here, Lieutenant? You're supposed to be in Deep!"

Captain Mandella's sharp tones came at her. It was just possible to detect a bottom note of sleepy endearment in the captain's voice. But you had to listen hard.

"Oh, nothing, Captain," Lieutenant Sky said, suppressing a wry smile.

"Then return to your sleepchamber, you dunderhead."

"Yes, Captain." Lieutenant Sky turned smartly, and headed out the Bridge doors.

Next waking shift, Lieutenant Sky called a formal group meeting. As Communicator, she could do that. The venue was Relax. Everyone was to attend, including the captain.

Sky stood in the centre of the room as they came in. Triple burrowed himself down into his favourite chair and looked studiously bored. Kaya entered, looking distracted. He took a chair near Triple. Shortly afterwards, the Captain entered, explaining to the Lieutenant that she'd been delayed by a faulty reading. She looked around, nodded perfunctorily to Officers Triple and Kaya, then stood in a corner, arms folded. Lieutenant Sky indicated that Mandella should take a chair, as the other two had

Mandella chose a high backed chair. She prodded the lavish cushioning disapprovingly, then sat.

All eyes were on Sky.

"What's this about?" Triple moaned.

She addressed them sternly.

"We are a team. And like it or not, we depend on one another."

"What's this about, Lieutenant?"

"Don't interrupt, Captain." Lieutenant Sky snapped.

Mandella was stunned into silence.

"In our three months together," Sky continued, "we have crossed galaxies, repaired stations in the remotest corners of the Cosmos, working in harmony. Until the Kayiga incident. Shit went down there and there's no point denying, or ignoring or playing that down and I'm not trying to."

She'd used an expletive. None of them had heard her swear before. They kept schtum as Sky surged on:

"...but we survived. Some of us have been forgetting that. We survived. And we can come through and be stronger as a team, if we want to." She paused looked at each of them in turn. "But do we want to?"

None dared look away as she continued.

"There are more than six months of this tour left. That's a long time to be harbouring grievances. A long time not to be talking to one another. You do not hate one another. You are trying very hard to hate one another, but you do not hate one another. Now speak up. Tell me if I'm wrong."

There was silence.

"Captain Mandella, you feel we let you down. We apologise, all of us. Sky turned to the two others and prompted them with a look that would brook no refusal.

Triple spoke up.

"Sorry, Captain."

"Keep your sorries," Captain Mandella replied to him subduedly, "just don't mess with the ForceCode again."

"Yes, Captain," said Triple. "Are we forgiven?"

Captain Mandella looked at Triple's penitent face and was minded to forgive. But what of Kaya? Officer Kaya had not offered any apology. She glanced at him. The rocketsman had his head down, tuned out. The bristling hostility she'd felt coming from him ever since the Kayiga Incident had gone. Only now could she see past her own fear long enough to notice. And she found herself, as Sky had said, finally not hating him.

"This one time, for the sake of harmony," Mandella said, "I'll forget what happened. I am willing to forget."

"Does that mean no more drills?" said Triple.

Mandella smiled then at him, for the first time in a long time. "I'll try ease up on them, Officer Triple."

She looked across at Kaya. "Officer Kaya, I'm sorry about your parents. If I had believed it was possible, I would have tried…"

"You've said enough, Captain," Kaya interrupted, "the bitter remember. The generous forget."

"How do you mean?" asked Mandella.

"It's a Kayiga saying," said Kaya.

Lieutenant Sky asked him to explain it and Kaya replied that it meant Kayigans did not harbour grievances. Then Triple jumped up and asked something else about Kayiga, and Mandella followed with a supplementary question about his parents. Kaya spoke at length like rain after a drought. Lieutenant Sky looked on and sighed.

That session they finally talked with one another, sharing their hurts, their hopes. It was a time of pure spirituality. And when the talking finally ended, Sky spoke softly.

"I propose a grief ceremony in honour of Officer Kaya's parents. Officer Kaya, will you help me prepare it?"

Kaya nodded.

"It will not be compulsory," Sky said, "but I hope everyone can find the time to attend."

Kaya gazed out of the meditation room porthole and remembered.

He had taken three keepsakes from his personal effects cache and arranged them on the plinth in the meditation room for the ceremony. Just three: a pearlised pill-box containing two tight curls of his mother's hair; a holograph of all three of them together when he was five Urth years old (they were swinging him through the air and he was yelling with delight in his ocean blue corduroy trouser bibs and red, white and green beanhusk jumper); and one long dried middle leaf from the hybrid plant his father had first created, Dokaya cannabis sativa.

Sky supplied a small, Tibetan brass bell.

Everyone attended.

They sat as Kaya described the significance of each object in turn before passing it round. He told them stories of his upbringing, said his parents had loved nature, loved the trees of Urth, the rivers of Kayiga, the birds, the insects, even the smallest microbe. They believed the same spirit that was in human beings was in the rains of Venus, and in the suns and moons of SunOne. On death, they had taught him, the human spirit joined the spirits of the stars, moons, rivers and trees. His parents lived on in these objects, but also all around him. They had been good teachers. They had taught him the duty of allsentient living beings was to transcend and uplift, by deed and by contemplation.

After that they'd sat together on the deep cushions of the meditation room in silence. For three minutes nobody stirred. There was just the sound of their breathing. When he finally felt ready, Kaya picked up the tiny brass bell from the plinth and rang it softly, to signify the end of the ceremony.

Three days later, and Kaya was gazing through the meditation room porthole remembering. The thought that his parents were dead still caused his fingernails to stab into his palms. But, like stardust clearing, he could see through and beyond that grief. And occasionally, like now, he could look back, and remember the pure, communing times he'd enjoyed with them.

From Sky's private log

Other people are our hell and our affirmation. The art of

relating is the art of acknowledging our sameness while respecting and understanding our differences. The material dimension is the simplest. The most beautiful object is just that — an object. But the ebb and flow of emotions, the cross currents of sympathies and hostilities are much more subtle and difficult phenomena. How hard they are to predict, to gauge, to record. So with Kaya. The phases of grief and anger and blame have passed with him. He appears to have reached true acceptance of his parents' death. He no longer blames Captain Mandella. We all witnessed his emotion during the Ceremony. It has united us as crew in a way we have not known before. We are keenly aware of our interdependence, of our mortality, and of our individuality. Particularly, I find Captain Mandella more beautiful for this, every day. I see her making this great effort to connect. She now radiates benevolence. There is rigour still, in the ship routine she imposes, and in formal interaction. But there is also greater harmony. Aura have normalised. Sleepdeficits are at zero. Interpersonal communication on zsf is good. We are closing on Planet Thuli.

The young heal fastest. Day Circadian 139: Shift Two found Triple in Relax, doing a Vurt workout. A masharikiragga beat came through the headsphere earzones. A Vurt posse of workout girls graced his headsphere screen. The Vurt girls were wholly interactive. As he danced, they mirrored his moves, and cheered him on to boot.

Sweat cascaded down Triple's back and he took off his outer tunic. The Vurt workout girls took off theirs. He liked that. He wanted to go naked so they would, but he was in Relax, not the Pleasure Store, so, reluctantly, he kept his underkit on. He got working — jacking, . And the workout girls kept up with him. The Vurt posse's collective pheromene, drenched sweat smell was being pumped by the headsphere into his nostrils. Triple was flying high.

Soon he had an audience. Sky had gone past, noticed, brought Kaya. Reading the desire patterns of his alpha brainwaves, Triple's headsphere screen tiled to offer him a choice: carnival, or dancehall girls? He chose dancehall. The beat upped. The Vurt girls closed in on him, bogling low. Sky and Kaya cheered him on. They could guess from his moves what was showing on his head sphere.

The noise attracted Captain Mandella. As a rule, Mandella didn't enter Relax. It was the crew's space, not hers. This once, she broke her rule. She leant on Sky's shoulder as the three stood together and laughed at Triple. Triple was blissed, euphoric. He knew he had an audience and he played up shamelessly to them. Strutting his stuff with the posse.

It was such a simple pleasure, Mandella thought, dancing. It reminded her how young Triple was. Had she herself ever danced? She couldn't recall. Still, as she walked back along the corridor to the Bridge, she tried a little skip of her own.

They were closing now on their destination. On the Bridge, Captain Mandella gave the order and zsf-e5 slowed to Mach 3.

"Officer Triple, do we have all-clear?"

From way up in his Gunnery look-out post, Triple commsed. "Yes, Captain, the sky's quiet. Total hush."

"Lieutenant Sky, have Thuli space control registered our orbit?"

"Yes Captain." Lieutenant Sky put the Thuli transmission on loudspeak for Mandella:

"-shib shum sham shap shab shep schum schum schum qua qua... Shib shum sham shap shab shep schum schum schum qua qua.."

"And what does that mean, Lieutenant?"

"They are ready for us to dock," Sky said hesitantly.

A quirk of spacetime travel was that time slowed down on board a spacecraft travelling at ultrahigh speeds. One year on board zsf was equal to fifty years on Planet Thuli. The last time Sky had called at Thuli was two ship years ago — a hundred years in Thuli time. So, although Lieutenant Sky had learnt the basic Thuli language, QuaQua, very recently in ship time, in Thuli time, like any other language, QuaQua had moved on. Sky had to use all her knowledge of predictive linguistics to comprehend the on-going communications.

Mandella saw her intense concentration.

"Are you steady on that, Lieutenant?"

"I'll originate one last time."

Sky repeated the request-to-land protocol. The transmission came through again. This time she was absolutely sure.

"Yes, Captain. They're expecting us."

"Thank you. Officer Kaya, prepare for descent routines."

"Yes, Captain."

"Collapse solar sail."

"Sail collapsed," Kaya replied.

"Close temperature control louvres."

"Louvres closed."

"Ozone check."

"Spectrometer reads OK."

"Magnetic field check."

"Magnometer on steady."

"Radiation check."

"Scintillation counter reads tolerable."

"Cosmic ray check."

"Cosmic rays absent…"

Although she had never called here before, Mandella had read the briefing on Planet Thuli thoroughly. It was a pretty standard planet, similar in atmosphere to the Solar System One's planet Mars. Thuli, like SunOne's Mars, had no great mass, and its mantle was correspondingly thin. Its natural atmosphere was argon, plus some nitrogen, plus even less carbon dioxide. Water existed down there, but there was little natural oxygen. Consequently, almost a sixth of Thuli's land mass was covered in a special gene-tricked wheat plant which converted carbon dioxide to breathable oxygen at a superordinary rate. It was this plant which effectively allowed aerobic life on Thuli. But the wheat down there was incapable of generating sufficient oxygen for long term sustainability. So the space force delivered every fifty Thuli years. The Zimbabwe Space Force oxygen delivery was Thuli's lifeline.

"Appoint propulsion nozzles," called Mandella.

"Nozzles appointed," Kaya responded.

"Unhitch cargoes two through five." Only the first cargo load was for Thuli. The rest could orbit until they were done on Thuli.

Cargoes two through five unhitched," Kaya confirmed.

"Descend five hundred metres."

"Descended five hundred."

"Heat shield status?"

"Heat shield status is good."

"Lock heat shield."

"Heat shield locked."

"Cargo shields configured?"

"Cargo shields configured and tight."

"Cargo shields configured?" the Captain repeated, a trace of her old annoyance returning to her voice. Officer Kaya had to use the exact protocol, and only the protocol. He knew that.

Kaya heard the Captain's annoyance.

"Cargo shields configured," he said precisely.

"Cargo seals tight?"

"Cargo seals tight."

"Place engine air filters on max."

"Engine air filters placed on max."

"Engine air pressure monitors active?"

"Engine air pressure monitors active."

Mandella scanned her dais instrument array. It all looked good. They were preparing to plunge into Thuli's atmosphere. The air pressure monitors would be vital. They were barometric switches and would fire zsf's retro thrust rockets to pull them out if the atmosphere readings became abnormal. The filters too were an absolute necessity, given the atmospheric conditions they would encounter.

"Routine accomplished," she said finally. "All satisfactory. Crew prepare for descent."

She watched them a moment as they donned pressure suits. She was already suited herself. Every Captain knew descent was the second most dangerous manoeuvre after take-off. She looked hard through the membrane at Thuli's clouds. There was an uppermost band of blue cloud composed mainly of argon. Then, clearly visible though breaks in the blue, a layer of white cloud which she knew to be ice crystals. Below that there would be a yellow haze which the probes said was wheat chaff stirred up by Thuli's winds. The filters would be maxed for that. The descent would be deliberately slow. When they made it through Thuli's mantle, they would dock, pump the oxygen and be away again. Mandella didn't want to linger there.

Beyond the dais, Triple was helping Kaya suit up.

"That Kieran must have been well randy, nuh Bones?"

"He sowed nuff wild oats," Kaya said, "where's the arm?"

"You mean wheat!"

"Yeah... plenty of that stuff down there too."

"Can't wait to get down there. Sounds like a good place to lose some more of my virginity."

"You taken your libido tablets recently?" Kaya asked. Triple was moving round him checking all his straps and fasteners were secured.

"Yes, Pops," Triple shot back, "handful a day. Guess you don't need them any more?"

Playfully, Kaya made to cuff him and Triple ducked.

"Now get us down in one piece, seen?" Triple said.

"This one's a hohum" Kaya said. He sat down and switched on his comms.

"Suited?" Mandella quizzed from her dais.

She got three affirmatives.

"Seat straints on max?"

Another three affirmatives.

"All right. Officer Kaya, take us down."

Kaya dipped the nose of zsf and they all felt the little kick as the ship plunged at the perpendicular into Thuli's stratosphere. Zsf's bridge membrane was soon obscured by cloud. Kaya guided them in using the instrument readings.

"Watch the filters," Mandella cautioned.

Kaya checked. They were functioning smoothly.

They broke from blue cloud into white and Kaya reined in the engines, letting Thuli's gravity do the work. Presently, they burst into the band of yellow cloud.

"Ease descent," Mandella commanded. The filter clearance mechanisms had to be given the chance to do their job.

Kaya tweaked the engines to slow zsf further. Then checked the filtration systems. They were cool, not even at half capacity.

The yellow cloud thinned and they were through.

As his adrenalin level subsided, Kaya put the ship on hold, circling the docking bay.

Triple unstrapped himself. He bounded over to Kaya. "Watcha Bones! Sweet flying!"

"I do my best."

"Listen to this, listen to this," Triple buzzed. "How many humans does it take to change a lightbulb?"

"Tell it!" he groaned.

"Six. One to do it, five to review it!"

Kaya shook his head.

"Sad."

Triple grinned ear to ear. "You better get used to it!"

Kaya supposed the kid was right. Thuli puzzled him. Myth had it that the patrolman who had first landed on Thuli during early exploration, had broken a cardinal ForceCode rule. A geneticist by trade, he'd cloned himself. Then stayed and brought up his offspring.

By the time another zsf craft landed, he'd established a sizable clan of Kierans. Kaya admired Kieran's chutzpah in outthinking Command Control. Human life being sacrosanct, Command had had to roll with it, even assist in the colonisation of Thuli by the Kieran clan. But they had severely punished Kieran himself, sentencing him to life isolation on a dead star-orbiting, punishment planet. Since he'd aged on Thuli, and was 96 Urth years by the time Command Control arrested him, the punishment was not in fact so severe. The reports said Kieran had died on the punishment planet two hundred Thuli years ago.

There were various embellishments on the myth. Most of them ribald. But nothing explained why Thuli had become a one-joke planet. Why did all Thulians repeat this one joke? The scientists put it down to an anomaly in the cloning process. Pilot Kieran had had only one joke in him, they explained, however he was spliced.

Whatever the answer to that conundrum, Triple was tickled by the irony of that Thuli joke. "Hey Kaya, how many humans does it take to change a lightbulb?"

"I just heard."

Triple reeled away laughing. "Didn't I say, you'd better get used to it?"

"Officer Triple!"

"Yes Captain?" Triple twitched. But instead of the blasting he'd anticipated, the Captain smiled.

"Tell me Triple, how many humans does it take to change a light bulb?"

Captain Mandella telling a joke. He'd never have known Sourface had it in her.

"Come on, you must know the punchline," she teased.

"Yes Captain."

"Say it then."

"Em.." Embarrassment froze his tongue.

"Six. One to do it, five to review it. Right?" Mandella said.

Triple nodded.

"We can leave that one to the Thulians now, then, agreed?" she said.

"Yes, Captain."

"Thank you. I like it when we can agree on things." Then she was busy with Lieutenant Sky. "What's the delay, Lieutenant?"

"No delay, Captain. They're just confirming we have compatible docking technologies."

Mandella wrinkled her nose. More likely the Thulians were running checks on their craft, she thought.

Eventually, they got their Go For Docking.They passed over plains of dustbowl red, then swathes of billowing yellow. Mandella watched Thuli City loom into view, a crystalline web of silver capped domes, bisected by the wide grey ribbon that was Thuli City's only river. Zsf-e5 reached as low as four hundred metres and the craft's sky-darkening cargo rumbled over the Thuli metropolis.

Kaya watched. Along the banks of the river, he saw the

silver banners of the Thuli plant-growing cloches referred to in the bioref logs.

Sky watched and imagined Thulians looking up at e5 in wonder. Perhaps they saw zsf as some dread, supernatural apparition. Liquid oxygen supplies came to them only once every hundred Thuli years. The sheer size of their cargo must impress and intimidate, she thought.

Zsf and its cargo roared on until they were over Thuli's barren red outback plains, where the intergalactic freight runway and its terminals were sited. Lieutenant Sky relayed instructions from Thuli control tower. They were to hold short of position G. Officer Kaya did one fly-past for atmospherics reconnaissance. The cargo made manoeuvring difficult. But all the instruments said it looked good. He took zsf into a touchdown dive.

Red oxide plains rushed up to meet them. He lifted zsf slightly at the last second, had the cargo touch down first. It was the cargo that would give trouble if there was going to be any. His finger hovered over the joystick's Cargo Jettison button.

The moment the cargo's riders touched the runway, its dedicated retro jets roared into action. A gigantic parachute catapulted from the rear of the cargo bulk. It filled and ballooned out. A small kick was felt in zsf. Officer Kaya acknowledged it and nursed down the relatively tiny e5 craft. The iron oxide runway surface was rougher than Kaya had expected. Making a mental note to examine the radar data again to see how he'd missed this, he opened out the shock absorbers to compensate, and fired the retro rockets harder. Zsf and cargo — engine and train — rumbled to a slow halt. He checked the cameras. They were just short of Position G. The cargo's mid-length was directly adjacent to the huge terminal's oxygen inlet pipe. Just as well, Officer Kaya considered. There would be no pushing back of this huge load.

The crew were demob happy. They'd unbuckled their seat restraints, were out of their suits and straining at the leash. As always Triple was the first with the verbals.

"Permission to drop foot on Thuli, Captain?"he buzzed.

"Permission denied."

Triple groaned.

The Captain panned her gaze around the Bridge. The others looked equally disappointed. It was the old sailors-on-leave syndrome.

"All right," she relented, "everybody gets six Thuli hours shore leave!"

"But that's hardly—" Triple protested.

"It's almost a day, craft travel time."

"Ok-aay," mellowed Triple. He'd just have to cram everything he wanted to do into those six hours.

She called them to order.

"Remember we may be on Thuli, and you may be on leave. But you are all ambassadors of the Zimbabwe Space Force. Conduct yourselves accordingly."

"When are you going to open the hatch, Captain?" said Kaya impatiently. They had six hours. And he and Triple still had to sort out the oxygen unloading before they could be off.

"Please," Mandella chided, "I have to recite you Leave Briefing. It's the regulations. You've been around long enough to know that, Officer Kaya."

"Couldn't you skip a bit?" Kaya asked. He'd heard the same briefing so many times it dented his head.

Mandella shook her head and soldiered on.

"You are ambassadors but you will be subject to the jurisdiction of the Thuli people. Remember your manners. If you are detained, I might have to leave you behind. The schedules are tight."

"Yeah, yeah," said Kaya quietly. That last was untrue. None of them could ever be left behind. The ship was undercrewed as it was.

"Call out if any of you have not I repeat, have not, taken the following:vitamin injection? glucose injection? six hour nebulisers? oxygen timed release implants?" There were no call-outs. "Good. Wake up, Kaya, I'm finished. Remember to step slowly through the irrade shower on exiting. Tidy your consoles first."

They grumbled, but got on with it.

Then Sky was by Mandella's side. Captain Mandella asked, and Lieutenant Sky agreed that she, Sky, would do the official diplomatic tour.

"You won't be lonely all by yourself on the ship?"

Mandella smiled wearily.

"I'll enjoy the solitude. You tread the carpets for me."

"Yes, there is peace in solitude," nodded Sky, and she went quietly back to her console.

As Sky moved off, Mandella called out to Triple. His big feet bounded over in three strides.

"Yes, Captain?"

"Officer Triple, Zimbabwe Space Force has invested thirty two millions in your training."

"Thank you, Captain."

"Command Control wouldn't like it if I lost you."

"That's your way of saying you care about me, right, Captain?" said Triple.

Mandella couldn't help but smile back. "If it makes you happy to think that, then yes... Look after yourself out there."

"Sure, Mom!" He turned on his heels before she could react.

She let him go. She waved over Officer Kaya. He came lamely. He knew what she was going to say. She said it.

"Young Triple needs a minder."

"And I'm up for the job?"

"That's right."

"No-can-do. I've got experiments to conduct."

"It's his first shore leave. You know how it is on these first leaves."

"The vegetation here is unique to this galaxy. And the soil."

"A discreet watch."

"I'm not babysitting him."

"It's an order, I'm afraid." Mandella motioned to her dais and the banks of screens it contained. "I'll be following you on the tag monitor. I expect to see your echoes close together on the screen."

"But he's all grown up — he's twice as big as me," Kaya scowled.

"Do you remember your own first shore leave, Officer Kaya. It's in the logs. Perhaps I can remind you."

"All right, all right. I'll babysit."

"Thanks for your co-operation, Officer Kaya," Mandella said slyly.

Five minutes later, Officers Triple and Kaya clambered down zsf's ramp. Triple was surprised to be helped off the last step by a Thulian. A female, he noticed with excitement, and in her very early twenties, smiling warmly at him. She was a little smaller than him, well-built and wearing rough-woven flaxen overalls. She had pink and white skin. Her long red hair was tied back in a tail. He shook her hand. It was firm and yet soft. He grinned back, already blissed.

Kaya made it down unaided and the Thulian proffered him her hand. Kaya shook brusquely. They had less than six hours, and he wanted the unloading done fast. The Thulian spoke as the handshake ended.

"I'm Kieran High Seven. We're bloody glad you could make it, friends. The air here's thinning badly. Unlike your midriff, Officer Kaya!"

Triple giggled.

Kaya glared. "I expected a mechanic, not a clown."

To Triple's dismay, the Thulian's voice became serious. "My apologies. I am the mechanic."

Kaya concentrated a moment, looking over the huge flying behemoth overshadowing them. Then he addressed the Thulian. "We need to unroll the hosing, one, match up the flange connection seals, two, seal, lock the seals, three, then start pumping, four. The entire cargo will need stabilising first though. And the jet shields pulling back. Do you have cranes ready?"

"Everything is primed," Kieran One Seven replied. "I'll take you to Hosing Storage."

They followed her under the cargo. The undercarriage

wheels alone were a good twelve times their size.

"Tell me about your entertainment here," Triple burst out, "I've heard it's wild!"

A rude twinkle lit the Thulian's eye.

"Later," she said to him. "First we've got work to do. Correct, Officer Kaya?"

"Correct." Kaya was three steps behind them, looking fierce,

as the Thulian led them to Hosing Storage.

He could see the extra spring in Triple's step as he walked beside the Thulian female. Now he saw the sense of the Captain's 'babysitting' orders. Sex outside of Sun Galaxy was not approved of by Command Control. Though protected blow jobs were OK. A typical Command distinction. He turned his mind to things mundane. The oxygen outlet hosing needed rolling out.

There was only one vehicle and only one Thulian. She appreciated this absence of pomp. Some planets laid on processions of thousands and banquet after banquet and exhausted you. Not Thuli it appeared.

The lieutenant descended the short flight of steps from the zsf Bridge. Her host was an androgynous-looking male, dressed in a loose, natural fibre chemise and thick cream pantaloons, strapped with a matching belt at the waist. His smooth features said late twenties. He had a big mouth, a riot of red hair cut short, and a fluffy red moustache over full, upward curling lips. He was tousling his hair with his big hands as she stepped down. He greeted her in tradQuaQua:

"I'm Kieran Five Five. Please call me Five Five, I'm your host."

"Deeply honoured Lieutenant Sky, second in command of zsf-e5. We apologise for our rushed landing," said Sky.

"Apologise nothing! Command control still sending you to all kinds of crazy ports?"

Sky looked up at him. There was a lop-sided grin on his face.

"Go on, you can tell me."

"You could say that," she chuckled.

"What do you call us? Planet Kieran, still — the one-joke planet?"

"No, Planet Thuli," Sky replied diplomatically.

The stepped into a small beetle shaped hoverpod, and he told her they were headed for Thuli metropolis. Five Five did most of the talking during the drive.

"Last time I played host I had President Qing from Planet Sula to show around."

"And now it's just little me?" Sky jested.

"You'll be more fun. That Qing, she was full of airs and graces. A real skimbrain. Not like you e5ers!"

Sky was baffled. Surely the current crew hadn't been together long enough to have a reputation? Unless news of the Kayiga misadventure had spread. Mandella would hate that.

"You tired, lieutenant?"

"Not really. Why do you ask?"

"You just went quiet on me."

Sky smiled. "I'm sorry. I'm not the galaxy's greatest conversationalist."

"That's OK. We'll reach into the metropolis soon."

They drove on in silence.

Sky looked out of the pod's front windscreen. Visibility was good. She could see for kilometres ahead. The sky was yellow with clouds and dappled blue. On the horizon was the bright silver shimmer of the metropolis. The road before them was smooth, wide and red. To each side were the barren red oxide plains, where light winds occasionally moved the dust to a swirl. There were no buildings on these plains and no signs of settlement. Occasionally another craft passed them going in the other direction, or even overtaking on their left or above. She guessed Five Five was driving slowly for her sake. The craft windows were wound half down, and a warm, thin air played about the pod interior. Her thoughts turned to Captain Mandella. The Captain was alone on zsf. Of all the crew, Mandella was the one most tired, the one who most needed rest. There was nothing more dangerous to the welfare of crew than tiredness in its captain. She had persuaded Mandella to rest, while she Sky did the official duties. She hoped the Thulians did not take it as a slight.

"Your planet is beautiful," Sky ventured.

"Thanks. We forget that sometimes."

"Does everyone live in the metropolis?"

"Yes. The red plains you see around you are uninhabitable. The soil's highly acidic. We're testing for micro-orgs that can break it down. No luck so far."

"So how is the metropolis different?"

"How do you mean, lieutenant?"

"How are you able to live there, but not out here?" She wasn't so much curious as making an effort at conversation.

"Oxygenation," Five Five replied. "But it's costly. So far we've only been able to colonise a small area. But when the reactor's built, things will change fast."

"You're going nuclear?"

"Wheat oil can only get you so far."

"That's your current energy source?"

"Yes. And solar panels. But it's not enough."

Suddenly Sky felt a sharp stab in her neck.

"Sha!"

"Did I say something?"

"A sting," Sky cried.

She reached up to her neck. But Kieran Five Five caught her arm.

"Stay still!" He'd pulled the pod up. Still holding her raised arm, Kieran leant over her. She could feel his breath on her neck. "It's a baby ditchfly," he said at last. "A mutant at that. I'll get it." He raised his hand to her neck. A brawny, smooth forearm came across Sky's face as he reached over. She felt his fingers take hold of a fold of her neck skin and pinch. "You have to squeeze the probes out too" he was saying. The pinch turned into a sharp pain.

"You're hurting me," she cried.

"Sorry." He wasn't long. Then he showed her the ditchfly between his fingers. He had it by its wings. It looked like an overweight Urth dragon fly, but with four sharp barbs at the tip of its head.

"Nasty little things," he said. "If you swat them, the probes hook into the flesh and pump in larvae. The larvae hatch in your lungs and fly out of your mouth. In between the hatching and the flying, they kill you of course." He

70

squished the fly between his fingers then looked at her again. He was grinning that lopsided grin.

"What's so funny?"

"Excuse me, lieutenant but I have to get the poison out." Before Sky could protest he'd ducked back under her chin had his mouth at her neck and was sucking.

"But! she protested. Then relaxed, went with it. His lips pressed hard into the folds of her neck. As he sucked, she thought, whimsically, that it was ages since she'd last had her neck sucked. Since Hugo in fact. The Thulian's body scent was of wheat and decanted fruit. Sky found it not unappealing. Despite herself, she felt a tingle of pleasure. Yes, Hugo had been a passionate necksucker.

"Are you finished yet?" she remonstrated.

Finally, the Thulian released her. He grinned with pursed lips, then turned, leaned over the driver's side window and spat a steady stream of red liquid out into the road.

"I think I got it all," he said. He was still smiling, her blood thinly on his lips. "Did you have injections before you disembarked?" her host asked smoothly.

"Yes" Sky said. She'd felt invaded. She didn't understand why. "In accordance with your own recommendations." Her anger cooled as fast as it had risen. "Thank you for the prompt first aid," she managed. He was smacking his teeth with his tongue, about to spit again.

"All part of the job," Five Five smiled. He spat. Pink this time, not red. He strapped himself back in. "And before you ask, lieutenant, no, I don't make a habit of sucking strangers' necks."

Sky laughed then. The red oxide gave way to pitch black soil. Traffic got heavier. The skyline broke up into individual buildings. These were tall — ranging from five storeys and one hundred metres high, to ten and twenty storeys. The buildings' silver, geodesic dome canopies glittered a welcome. Soon glass-reed mesh buildings towered on either side. There was nobody around. Only a few bald headed youths lingered, with wail-boxes pumping out strange noises. One shouted at them, spread all four fingers out and moved his arm up and down. Five Five noticed Sky shrink.

"Ah, our gilded youth. Have your people at Command Control found a way of by-passing the human adolescence stage yet?"

They passed walking Thulians here and there, all dressed similarly to Five Five. There seemed to be no clothes dye available yet on Thuli. Either that or it was a very conformist culture.

"You look thirsty," said Five Five. "There's a place on the other side of town where we can drink."

"I want to see the river first."

"It's not really on the route."

"I can't see it?"

"It's nothing special."

"But I want to see it."

"It's like any other river, except maybe slower…"

She persisted.

"You really want to see it?… The river it is then."

Daylight hours on Thuli were shorter than Urth hours, and though only an hour had passed since zsf-e5 landed, the Thuli sky was darkening by the time they reached the river. Sky got out of the hoverpod and asked to be allowed to make the short walk to the banks alone. Request granted, she ventured from the pod, and stood on the river's left bank, taking in the sight. The heavy waters lapped at her feet.

She was upset and needed calming and rivers did that for her. She loved rivers. The way they were always changing and yet were always the same. The way they drew lifeforms to their bank, nursed civilisations. Rivers were a meditation for the mind, a psalm for the soul. With their unknown depths, their hidden strengths, they were metaphors of potential. Their rise and fall, ebb and flow, were naturally hypnotic. To sail a river was to be in touch with Urth, air and water all at once. It was a primal joy Sky felt, watching rivers like this. A river could move her to tears. She stood on the left bank alone, contemplating the slow moving waters. The image of the dark yellow sky swirled in the river's deep red surface. It had a wide girth and moved sluggishly, like cooling lava heavy with metal particles. It was an old river, making a stately passage through the young Thuli metropolis buildings that clung to its banks. When she died, Sky wanted her ashes to be sprinkled into a river, as the ancient Urth Hindus had given their dead to their Holy River Ganges.

"It's a beautiful thing, isn't it?"

She turned. Kieran Five Five had joined her. The tone of his voice, a mixture of reverence and vague spiritual longing, reflected Sky's own mood exactly.

"Yes," she said softly. She spoke no more. Just drank in the river's majesty, the tranquillity of the moment. Finally she said, "I guess we should be going." It was very dark now, and he took her hand to guide her, and they moved off the riverbank, back to the pod.

He took her to Glug. It was a metropolis bar. Here there were ordinary people, not the senators and pearl-tongued political spinners she and Mandella were usually sequestered with.

"Have a guess what they serve here?" Five Five was saying, as they settled into their bar stools.

"Wheat beer?"

"You been here before then?"

Lieutenant Sky smiled, and looked around as Five Five ordered. Glug had a high dark ceiling and curved opaque glass walls on which sand-coloured mood patterns softly rose and fell. Muted conch shell riffs created a mollifying acoustic. A smell of brew lingered. They were sat at the main, long, blonde bar. Beyond this was a scattering of tables and chairs. Dotted around were a few quiet customers.

Their drinks arrived in four long necked glasses. Five Five pushed two towards her.

"Why two at once?"

"It's about to get crowded."

Her mouth was parched from the wheat dust and she sank her first glass, way down to the bottom in one long, pleasurable gulp. The beer was sharp. She closed her eyes and followed its chill course from the back of her throat to her stomach. It was ultrapotent. When she looked up again a twenty-strong crowd was storming Glug's entrance arch. They were like a different tribe. A macabre cast of Thuli's scammers, slackers, shirkers, bruisers, barkers and miscreants. Their chemises were patched and their scruffy pantaloons held up with coarse string. The men were stubbled and groin scratching. The women were bedraggled. They pressed their armpits into her face at times as they shouted to the overworked bar staff. And they were chucking the beer down their throats. Maybe these Thulians had developed a resistance to the stuff. The high stench of sweat, and the acid wheat beer smells made her nauseous. She was afraid she would vomit and upset her host.

"What do these people do?" she bellowed, her mouth pressed almost to his ear.

"Dredgers, breakers, chaffers," he yelled back, "a few planters and croppers. Thuli's labourers. At the end of the day they've built up a thirst Are you comfortable? — we can leave if you want."

"I'm fine," Sky lied.

Truth was, she had not been among such sweaty slobbiness, such beery garrulousness, since the days of the Great Solar System Five Peace Celebration — yes, that great misnomer — which was all of twenty three of her years ago; and even then she had never got as unsober as these Thulians. Their wild energy shocked her. She contrasted the scene with the calm of zsf-e5. The craft's pristine environment and carefully regulated routine suddenly seemed very precious to her.

A fight broke out, not two metres from where they were sat. Five Five grabbed Sky's arm and steered her away from the fracas. The locals hurried forward. Cheers went up as the fighters sprawled onto the Glug floor. They were slugging it out nose to nose. One of them knocked the other over. The tall, twisting heap of a man, his face already splashed with blood from a broken nose, jumped on his felled opponent and straddled the shorter, barrel-shaped man, the better to apply the strangle hold he had on his neck. The shorter man bucked and thrashed on the floor. The tall man grinned. The neck hold stayed. The short man's body jerked into a bridge. His huge belly arched upwards and the taller man was thrown off him. Now it was the short man's turn to grin inanely.

"You're finished, conehead," he said in QuaQua. Suddenly the short one stopped and turned. His face showed surprise. "Who's she?" he bellowed.

There was a sudden, cold silence. All eyes followed the accusing finger. It was pointing at Sky.

"I'm Sky, I came with zsf — e5 — the oxygen supply ship." she said in QuaQua.

There was a murmur from the crowd. The tall man used the lull to get back up on his feet. Now he moved to the short man's side. The short man was still pointing.

"Who asked the alien here?" he asked accusingly.

Five Five stepped forward. "I did, Ugly. You want to argue with me on that?"

Five Five's face was lit with an easy, taunting smile. Both brawlers were looking at him, weighing him up almost professionally. The crowd stayed tight. Sky sensed their bloodlust. She must have done something wrong.

"Do you want me to leave?" Sky asked her accuser. "If it makes you happier, I will, it's no trouble."

"Mmm," said the short man, his jowls working as if he were sloshing her words like wheat beer around his mouth. "You know what would make me happier?" he smiled, showing his crooked teeth.

"Tell me. If I can help I will."

"This!" He swivelled fast, bent at the knees, and punched his huge fist hard into the lower abdomen of the tall man beside him. The tall man tottered. The fat man kicked him in the same place as he'd punched and he fell and the fat man jumped on top of him, fists pummelling. The crowd were delirious, Lieutenant Sky and her companion completely forgotten.

Sky turned to Five Five and shouted above the fracas: "Why do they fight?"

"Those two always fight like this. Every workday. Nobody knows why. Least of all the two of them. You can set your watch by them. They're more boisterous than usual this time though. I think they're putting on a show in your honour."

Sky frowned,

"It's not my kind of show."

The yelling stopped. The fight broke up as suddenly as it had started. Sky watched the two men help each other up off the floor. She distinctly saw the tall one wink at her from across the room, as he walked with his buddy back to the bar. It was all a charade, she sensed. Though the blood was real, there was a game being played here, and somehow she was involved.

FIve Five rescued their remaining drinks from the crowded bar and managed to find space at one of the tables. "This one drink, then I want to leave." Sky said firmly to Five Five.

"So do I," he echoed.

She wasn't sure whether he was joking. Why had he taunted the thug by calling them Ugly? Why had they fought? What would have happened if she'd not deflected attention from Five Five when she had? Despite his protestations, Five Five seemed to be in his element here. He was conversing with a young woman to his left. The woman's companion, sitting opposite her at the table, leaned over and introduced herself as a doctor of medicine.

"Me too…" Sky responded.

"I thought as much."

"Why's that?"

"The worry lines!"

Sky smiled.

"You're from the cargo ship aren't you?"

"Yes," Sky said.

There was a small silence between them then. The Thuli

doctor was dressed in a loose cut, flaxen gown that was tied at the waist. She had blotchy red eyes and thin, long fingered, well manicured, venous white hands. There were five empty, long necked glasses and one full one before the Thulian medic on the table.

"Your hospital work you hard?" Sky chanced.

"No, not particularly…"

Sky looked at her.

"You looked troubled."

"Can I ask you a question, physician to physician?"

"Of course."

The medic leaned over further so Sky could smell the wheat on her breath.

"I have two patients. One a baby of six weeks. The other a poet of sixty years. Both are dying. We have only enough serum for one. Which do I save?"

"I'm sorry. I can't help you." Of course, given zsf-e5's superior equipment and greater medical knowledge, in all likelihood, she, Sky, would be able to heal them both. But such intervention was forbidden by Command Control on policy grounds. And her own value judgments on who should survive would not help the young doctor. Each social system had to evolve its own ethics. What was morally right in one galaxy could be disastrously wrong in another. No matter that Thuli was populated by humans.

"It's a tough decision,"Lieutenant Sky sympathised to the doctor.

"One I can only make myself, right?" The Thulian said it with a dour smile.

Five Five was nudging her. "It's time to go," he called.

Sky stood. "My thoughts are with you, doctor," she said.

"That's what we say to people here when they're dying — my thoughts are with you."

"I'm sorry. I didn't mean… I meant I have to go." She felt stupid. Had she offended the doctor? "It was good meeting you," she said and walked awkwardly away.

When they reached outside a chill air blew. They huddled together as they made their way to the pod. The beer had woozied her head a little.

"It was good to meet real people," she said.

"I thought you'd enjoy it," Five Five said.

"Where now? No crowds though, please. I find them stressful."

"No crowds," he promised.

He was holding her arm in the crook of his own.

Sky felt good. She had warmed to Kieran Five Five. The Thuli sky was a deep cobalt blue. She looked up, imagined the cargo train orbiting, up there in Thuli's stratosphere. What would Mandella be doing now? Would she be at rest — in deep and full-dreamed, recuperative sleep? Mandella had hard-earned her time off. And she thought of Kaya and Triple. If Triple had to stick with Kaya, they would be out be discovering Thuli's flora and fauna, she speculated. Right now, Kaya might be poring over a handful of Thuli's wheat-bearing soil, or else peering with the aid of a flashlight at the hard red oxide minerals of the outback. Triple would be a volubly reluctant assistant. But they would get on. They always did. Planets were something special. Zsf-e5 visited more space stations and satellite towns than planets. So few planets were inhabitable. A few were inhabited but had environments too hostile for the human species. Sky's thoughts wandered on. It was strange how travel made you aware so much more intently of home. Customs that were taken for granted viewed from the distant perspective that space travel brings, quaint, or inspired, or laden with symbolic meaning. So how Urth dogs barked, how the schools shrank the human spirit, how the land was owned by corporations and individuals in perpetuity, how rainwater and oxygenated air were free on Urth, all these things were strange now. Also the Urth system of queuing, and rituals of dying, and the Urth words for feelings. From the millions upon millions of kilometres between Thuli from Urth, all these things seemed strange and novel.

"You look faraway," Five Five said.

"Just dreaming," she replied softly.

"Dreams are good for you." They were by the pod.

"Come on, get in."

She got in. Wave music filled the cockpit. He looked over to her. He was about to say something, but didn't.

Eventually she spoke. She was looking skywards:"What star is that, Five Five?"

"The Great Bear. Why?"

"Who gave it that name?"

"I don't know. Sounds better than AP1105-H I suppose."

"That's its map name?"

"Uhuh."

Sky gazed at the Thuli sky. All the stars pulsated. She was reminded of the vastness of the multiverse zsf traversed, the multiverse's cold order, and the precious, special warmth of human contact. Against the alienating infinities of space it was all they had — each other. And they created worlds in their own image, worlds that reflected that human need for warmth, and hung human labels on cold cosmic matter. So The vast Urth Galaxy became the loveable Milky way and the cartographer's star AP 1105H became the huggable Great Bear for Thulians. Her head rested on Five Five's shoulder. He put his arm around her, and she thought now, at this particular moment in time, how she loved the physical heat that transferred from Five Five's shoulder through his flax chemise to her cheek. She breathed in his body scent and welcomed his presence beside her. She was happier than she could remember.

The place he took her to was an apartment in one of the tall Dome buildings. The same ambient ocean music was playing. They ate snacks and drank water and she felt refreshed yet still dreamy, and she was glad they were alone together.

"More water?"

"No."

"Rusks?"

"I'm full. There's no food shortage here?"

"There's huge granaries brim-full. And thanks to you, we'll soon have oxygen on tap."

"I'm happy for you. You're vegetarians?"

"Yes. The ecosystem here is delicate."

She lazed in his arms.

"Sky…"

"Yes?"

"I'm very fond of you."

She looked up at him, not quite surprised. She meant to look away again swiftly but found that she couldn't. His eyes changed like a slow kaleidoscope as she gazed into them, picking up flecks of light green and lime until she found herself looking into Hugo's eyes. She saw Hugo's long black hair, Hugo's playful lips, his thick, corkscrew eyebrows, and his way of cocking his head to one side slightly… *Hugo.* But had he not died on board…?

He was opening out a hand to entwine it with hers. The tips of her fingers touched his palm. She felt the fingers. Felt the scar on the inside of the left small finger. It was Hugo for sure.

But then quickly, as if stung, she withdrew. No. This was not Hugo. And, trembling, with anger more than fear, she asked, "Why?"

The figure before her transformed. The hair, the eyes, all the features morphed. Kieran Five Five was before her again.

"I didn't mean to startle you," he said softly.

Her voice was hard. "Why?"

"Can I explain?"

"Make it good."

"I am a QuaQua. We QuaQua are reeders: multipersonality metamorphs, in your language. We can assume the guise of other species — become them in body and mind, while retaining our own parallel QuaQua selves. I learnt about you from the blood sample I took from your neck and from observing you. I used the information to change myself into the form of your soulmate, Hugo. "

"Your body now is a disguise?"

"If you like, yes."

"Then show me your real self!"

Five Five declined gently.

"Most human beings find QuaQuas too repulsive. You yourself, Sky, are not gifted to sight our natural form, despite your compassion. Likewise your Command Control. Their instinct if they saw us would be to attack us. We know this. But the man, Kieran was exceptional. He could sight us. And he allowed us to... copy him. We cloned human forms for ourselves for when we present to humans. But one man's sperm can offer only so many variables. We are close to exhausting all possible Kierans.

"When we learnt of your coming visit, we thought it would be an opportunity to replenish. We wanted — we need, to widen our understanding of humans, our range of human expressions. We had had several opportunities before zsf. But we wanted the right material, genes that would strengthen, not reduce us."

"How do you mean?"

"The Kieran genes have a flaw. A capacity for extreme violence is imprinted in them. You saw it this evening. We have been testing you. The fight at the bar was a test. The doctor's questions as well."

Sky was subdued.

"Did I pass?" she said sarcastically.

"Yes," Five Five said. "Will you help us?"

"You're speaking Urthnation language now."

Five Five shrugged.

"We are good linguists. We use QuaQua only because it is expected of us. You are upset. I'm sorry for deceiving you."

"Five Five, you are an arrogant shit!"

"Don't blame me. It comes from Kieran!"

She almost hit him, but couldn't bring herself to. Instead she found herself laughing. Five Five joined in. He had a rolling, squelching gargle of a laugh. It was the first time she had heard this laugh. The laugh of a QuaQua. But she was not afraid.

"Sky?"

"Yes?"

"You can help us to evolve."

She could sense him building up to something.

"How?"

"Will you… lie with me?"

"Are you suggesting you and I… ?"

"Yes. Please — don't rush to refuse. All we need is one ovum."

She shook her head, incredulous. "But I haven't ovulated for five years."

"The potential is there. I traced the hormones in your blood."

"Why would I suddenly ovulate — eight years after my menopause?"

"Upon deep orgasm, it can happen. I can give you that orgasm."

"You flatter yourself, Five Five!"

He smiled bashfully.

"Please, help us. You will enjoy it."

She was light headed.

"This is incredible."

"I promise you will enjoy it. Try not to feel guilty afterwards."

"Let me think." She moved away from him. *Sex with an alien? Why should she take such a risk?* Besides, why her, plain, old Sky. Surely they had asked the wrong person. And yet she saw their problem. And there was a possibility that good would come of it. Who knew, in years to come, how the QuaQuas might come to the aid of humans if she helped them now? Captain Mandella would say no of course, if she contacted her, would have ridiculed the whole thing, promise of deep orgasm included. But they weren't asking Mandella. She, Sky, had been chosen. And she, Sky, had to decide. She turned to him. "What if I do ovulate? What then?"

"I will take your ovum into my own organs where I already have Kieran's sperm and the QuaQua tamazoon. Nine months from now, our child will be born."

There were many things she didn't know. Many things she had to take on trust. But his aura was true and her instinct was yes, and she followed it. She nodded. She didn't feel like speaking now. He moved gently. There was a mattress he rolled out, and a blanket. He dimmed the lights to a soft glow. Turning her back to him, she removed her clothes. Then she lay down, and and covered herself; Five Five removed his clothes too, and lay with her.

"But please," she said to him, "don't be Hugo."

He kissed her left cheek below the eye and whispered he understood.

He was careful and attentive and slow. She clung to him, felt the ripples of soft pleasure as he rocked with her. She felt him enter her and gave a little groan. He was lying high on her and she closed her eyes and felt the rocking rhythm as he pushed gently further in. Waves of intense desire broke across her mind. She had had her eyes closed, but now she opened them and saw him and he was every man, every woman she had ever desired. She closed her eyes again and the lust for him was intense and she began moaning, moaning on the peak of every wave, and each successive wave that charged over her rose higher and higher before breaking, until the tidal wave came and she shuddered, clung, clasped, and had the first orgasm. He didn't sidle away then, as most of her men had.

He was still in her, rocking, and she felt faint. Her legs were clasped round his back, the heels digging, spurring; her hands, fingers stiff with desire, rubbed the back of his head.

She rocked with him.

Her moan became a pant. She wanted him to speed up now and she dug her heels in harder, pulled at his hair urgently. He began to thrust hard, still riding high on her. She felt herself shudder again and again, as she held him, guided him. And she could feel her body singing, her whole body sang out joyously as waves of bliss broke, overwhelmed her.

For a moment she lost consciousness.

When she came round she still felt faint, light-headed. Five Five's arm was cradled around her. As she stirred she heard him say, dreamily, "Thank you," as he stroked her.

"You…I…I never…"

"We chose well. You are beautiful," he said.

"What about this sailors' entertainment then?" quizzed Triple. He was tightening the last huge bolt on the oxygen pipeline.

"Our founder Kieran Kieran—"

"Yeah, randy Kieran!" chuckled Triple.

"Zip your lip, youth!" said Kaya.

"Our founder Kieran," One Seven continued unfazed, "said there are only three things astronauts are looking for when they park up during a tour."

"What're they?" asked Triple.

"One. They want drink. Two. They want drink."

"And three?" Triple pressed.

She laughed.

"And three. They want to get laid!"

"Can't say he got it wrong," Triple shot back.

Kaya looked at the junior sternly. Cleared his throat. "He put it that crudely?" he asked the Thulian.

"Was he wrong?" she said.

"Officer Triple, don't answer that!" He sensed she was toying with them. He gave the flanges one last inspection. Then checked the parachute was properly repacked. Everything was sound. The pumping routines were computer controlled. There were no further manual procedures to perform.

"A tough job well done," he said, more to himself than to them, standing back and admiring his handiwork.

"Looks solid," said One Seven. "Should last a good five years. Now. Do you two want to visit Thuli's lights?"

"Mmm. I've heard you have new crops growing. Superoxygenating edibles," Kaya stalled.

Triple glared at him. "What're you talking about?"

"Yes," said One Seven, replying to Kaya. "But the research farm is in the opposite direction to the city. There isn't time to visit both." She looked them each in turn. "So. Which is it to be?"

"The city!" Triple said unhesitatingly.

"The farm," countered Kaya.

"You two want to talk it over for a moment?"

"The decision's made. It's the farm."

"Speak for yourself!"

"Will you excuse us?"

Kaya drew Triple to one side. "Now listen—"

"No you listen!" Triple whispered.

"Don't be a dog!"

"I don't recall I took a vow of chastity among all the other oaths when I joined zsf! C'mon, Bones, you can't deny me this."

"You're junior to me. I can."

"There's no problem anyway. You make your way to the farm. Me and One Seven'll head for the city."

"If we split the captain'll see it on Trace."

"And who's afraid of her? Look, I can't stand around arguing. I got people waiting." He nodded over to One Seven.

Kaya seethed. He'd been keen to study the hydroponic systems. A chance to study such advanced systems as those on Thuli arose only once every tour. They were pioneering a revolutionary series of superoxygenating non-wheat food crops here. Rumours abounded. Now he had the opportunity to separate fact from fiction. Instead he was being asked to play condom-carrier to the young buck, to be a bit part player in a teens-get-laid movie. It puzzled Kaya, Triple being frisky as a dog in summer. All crew were issued anti-sex drive tablets. Maybe Triple had stopped taking them in readiness for the Thuli port call. It was a common trick. The big footed youth stood there sulking. All in all, he guessed he owed him. Compared with what Triple had risked for him over Dogon III, this would be a small favour.

"Well?" Triple was glaring at him.

Kaya cursed.

"You really are a dog, know that?"

"I can go?"

"Get in that thing!"

Triple clambered into the back of the pod. Kaya squeezed in alongside him.

One Seven started the vehicle off. It elevated, then advanced along the slip road onto the main highway.

"It's party time, Bones." Triple dug him in the ribs. "When was the last time you partied? I know you. You've forgotten how — am I right or am I right? But don't worry, Bones, me teach you!"

"That's why I'm worried," Kaya growled.

"C'mon! This is my first shore leave. Be happy for me."

"Woof, Kijana, woof."

"That's the spirit, Bones! Awooah!"

The pod had surged up in the air. Triple looked down and saw they had leapfrogged another pod.

"Excuse me, do you always drive like this?"

"Only when I'm sober!" One-Seven winked.

Triple leaned back.

"Ain't she funny?"

"Yeah. I'm kicking myself." Kaya strapped himself in.

"Cheer up, Bones. Things could be worse — we could be on Urth!"

With One Seven concentrating on driving, and Kaya in his mood, Triple occupied himself with looking out of the pod window.

Thuli was a perky planet — the sky was smiley yellow, and the deserts a blushed red. In the distance, the silver domes winked him a welcome. Soon they were in the midst of the domes.

"I'll take you around town. First the Happy Domes."

"Sounds good to me! What do you say, Bones?"

"The name's Kaya. And the rulebook says I call the shots

on leave outings."

"You got that rulebook on you?"

"I've memorised it."

"Memory has a habit of playing tricks on people. Especially old people."

"I know what I know," Kaya insisted "You go where I say. Nowhere else."

"Ok-aay, Officer Kaya. Message received. Now, can we go?"

"Yes," Kaya relented.

"May I address our host once more?"

"So long as you're not vulgar or disrespectful."

"I will do my best, Sir," Triple snorted in disgust. Kaya was becoming Mandella.

They entered a Happy Dome. There, with Officer Kaya holding back and shooting a range of disapproving looks at young Triple, the most junior officer of zsf-e5 got in touch with his party self. He drank the wheat beer, sang the Thuli drinking rhymes, and hug-danced with the Dome's clientele. He had soon learnt the footwork and armwaves for a dozen Thuli reels and rumbas.

Three Happy Domes later, even Officer Kaya was thawing. For the sake of diplomacy he explained to the junior officer, he would accept One Seven's invitation to do a short rubfest with her on the dancefloor. He found the effects of the rubbing sufficiently pleasing for his diplomacy to stretch to another dance with One Seven, and then one last one to cement the goodwill. He then drank three flutes of wheat beer to show willing.

It was dark, and Triple's legs were aching when One-Seven finally drove them to their last Happy Dome, the Eros Dome. She'd left it till last.

"You coming in, buddy?" Triple asked of Kaya.

Kaya shook his head.

"My soul is tired."

"I didn't know souls had sex."

"When the soul is tired, the body fails to get excited."

"You can't get it up? That's sad, old man." Triple made to

open the side door of the pod.

Kaya held his sleeve. "Remember the protection — you know where to put it on?"

"Yeah — my dick, right?"

"How?"

"I guess you unroll it so it's like a tube. Why can't I use the spray-on?"

Kaya sniffed. "Ozone's too fragile here." He held the young man's gaze earnestly. "Listen, Junior — you run into any trouble, just shout and I'll be right there."

"Yeah, Pops, thanks."

One Seven saw him to the door and Triple disappeared inside.

Kaya got out to stretch his legs. Ranked up there in the top ten of his all time Least Favourite Things To Be Doing was waiting around while someone else got laid. He caught a blast of technojazz and a shockwave of heat as the doors opened momentarily to admit the youth. The place was rammed and jumping. But he wasn't tempted. Soon, as he wandered up and down outside the dome, he imagined he could hear Triple's howls and yelps and oohs among the orgiastic sounds of the other clientele. Topping all these gutturals was the loudest live technojazz band he'd heard in three tours. Now he was tempted, but only to go inside and hear them play. They played with style on Thuli. One Seven was sitting in the pod driving seat, dozing. He went over to her, leaned into her window, shook her shoulder gently. She woke. "How long's he likely to be?"

"Two minutes!"

"That fast?"

"Pants off — horizontal — dick up — a couple of thrusts — he comes — he pays — he goes," she yawned.

"Yeah. Same everywhere, I guess."

"You don't fancy some rumpy?"

"I prefer plants."

She looked curious. "How do you have sex with them?"

"No—"

"Just kidding, Officer Kaya."

"Yeah."

Kaya wandered away again. Why everyone was so obsessed with sex was what he wanted to know. Or maybe it was him. Had the sexdoze tablets flattened his drive? Or was it symptomatic of his general bodily decline? He was old now. You had to surrender the things of youth: splurgeball, recreational drugs, looking in mirrors, idols, your own teeth, watching cartoons, Get Rich Quick dreams, and instant erections. With sex, he preferred memories to the real thing. The time with Limau in the loading bay on his first tour. They'd been fast and furious and done it at least fifteen times during the tour. Then the time with Deckshine on Kayiga. They two had flattened plenty grass rolling around. And Mwamerika. He and Mwamerika had gone through the Kama Sutra picking out positions one day. He'd had stamina then. And then there was Uzuri. His first big romance. They'd done everything together. He could still feel the stickiness of her hand in his. They'd run in the fields, swam naked in rivers. Bob-sleighed in the snow. Had natural sex in the dry, powdery soil of a maize field. She had worn an above-the-knee, red, crushed cotton dress. They'd gone swimming. He emerged from the water and she saw him aroused. She beckoned, slipped off her dress again. After the deed, they swore undying love to each other. He wondered about Uzuri. He knew she was now an Agronomist on Urth. He'd have to look her up one time when this tour ended.

Another yelp reached him from the Dome. Kaya mentally stuffed his ears with cotton wool. The act of fornication struck him as absurd. Two bellies rubbing together, lots of moaning, sighing, sweating, sliding. And the stupid things you said while doing it. It was a poor substitute for companionship. How much more satisfying was a decent, in depth discussion of, say, lichen growth rates, than two minutes frantic wriggling? He was sure Sky felt the same. With age comes a mellowing of passion, a blanching of life's colour, a fading of heart, a disillusionment of dream, a surrender into the grey (the grey

90

in his hair now, he knew, was almost more plentiful than the black). My bones creak, he said to himself, my body doesn't roar — it mutters and complains. I should wrap himself in the cloth of the middle-age: financial caution, moderation in all things, acceptance of limitations. He knew now he'd never make it to Command Control level, and that the epic love affair he'd been waiting for all his life was unlikely to happen for him. It hurt, this surrender of dreams. Meanwhile, while he was out here getting mawkish and feeling sorry for himself, young Triple was in there dipping it in and out!

★

Fast in her chair seat, feet up on the dais, hands intertwined behind her head, Captain Mandella was imagining the perfect conversation with her crew:

"Permission to practise more object verification routines, Captain?"

"Permission granted, Officer Triple, but don't overdo it. You've been doing three routines per shift already."

"Yes, Captain. But I enjoy it, Captain."

"Good for you."

"Captain?"

"Yes, Lieutenant Sky?"

"On behalf of all the crew, we'd like to say thank you for a tough job well done."

"Any particular reason for this announcement?"

"No. We just feel you should know."

"Well, I appreciate your remarks. I do my best for you."

"Captain?"

"You as well, Officer Kaya?"

"Yes. Captain, recognising the importance of proper deference to authority, and conscious of the bad example my behaviour set for those of tender minds — that's Triple here — I'd like to apologise for speaking out of turn last shift, Captain."

"Apology accepted, Officer Kaya."

Dream on, Captain Mandella thought wryly. Especially with an all-black crew. An all black crew thought they had a license to disrespect her more, because she was like them, black. That they were all Africans together was no coincidence. Command Control in their wisdom had arranged it. She herself was from the Southern sector, Officer Kaya came from the Associated Planetary Isles, Lieutenant Sky came from the Sudan zone of the North sector, and young Triple was YorAmerican. Mandella yawned, and as she tried to think of an upside to this she glanced at the tag screen. The three dots were moving away slowly and in the anticipated directions.

Suddenly she felt happy. And hungry. Food was the one big upside of an all-black crew. They could stock up on AfricanNation food. And now, with all the crew gone, she could raid the fridge big-time. Sauntering along the corridors, the craft seemed more airy, more spacious, cleaner without the rest of them. She felt the walls, loving the satin feel of the tiles. She felt free. And things that had been on the back of her mind for ages came forward at times like this. Like the number of times she'd seen Officers Triple and Kaya with the expression "go stuff yourself" in their eyes. Well, now she would stuff herself.

There was a limited amount of irradiated fresh food stocked on zsf. The Union had negotiated it for all crew. It supplemented the dried, pulverised and pelleted produce, which, when reconstituted, was their staple diet. The work routine was to take the prepack, water it, heat it, eat it, then bin it. Some of the fresh was ready-to-eat, but most wasn't. For that you needed to know how to cook. And of them all, only Captain Mandella did. Officer Kaya, for all his talk about Organics, couldn't steam a bamboo shoot. So it was all hers.

She entered the Galley, She opened the pantry door and scooped out the silver pack of Three Gorgons cheese. She bit through the silver and peeled it away. The aroma of fresh cheese assaulted her nostrils and nearly laid her out. She bit a chunk off. Bliss. Then another and another. She put it back.

The edge was off her hunger. Now she would cook.

After a burst of culinary improvisation the galley stove was heavy with a multitude of hot and half empty pots and pans, while Mandella sat at the galley table, tunic sleeves pushed up, eyes romancing the spread that lay before her. There was garnished Callaloo soup in a silver chased engraved tureen; nudging tíhe tureen was runaway turkey scallops in tangerine jerk sauce; further down the table was a zsf regimental platter on which jostled bulging, pimento stuffed aubergines, steaming black eye beans and rice, thick sliced, old Trinidad fried plantain. Almost beyond the reach of her arm was brown-sugared apple and mango in cream medley; and finally a carafe of Nile Valley rice wine, in a chased silver goblet. It was her Mandella Gets Stuffed Special. She was dining off the official guest silverware. And today's official guest, she decided, was herself.

"Welcome, Captain Mandella!" she burped to herself as she threw back the last drop of Nile Valley sake. "We are honoured to have you on board. By the way, what happened to your brilliant career?"

Another burp. "I don't know. A run of bad luck. Bad crews. Bad ships. Bad missions. What more can I say?"

"You were a contender once, remember? You were Command Fleet material."

"I still am a contender, fuck you, I still am!" She shut up a moment to get her tongue straightened out. Then wandered on: "I belong with Command. Not with zs effing f, lugging supplies through backspace on a muleship. Is that all I'm good for? Did I spend eighteen years being flash-carded and flung about at Flight Leadership Institute for this? I've got pedigree. My mother—" here she burped again and apologised, "my ovum mother, was the first black woman President of the Pan African Nuclear Foundation. My mother propounded the Second Theory Of Velocity. My grandma invented everlasting lightbulbs..." This last statement had been told to her by her own mother but it struck her now as slightly absurd, and she hesitated. Who was she talking to? Herself? High Command? Her conscience? Her ego? The ForceCode? The ForceCode had got it all of course, she thought. Well, Omm could take it all in, file it, comms it network-wide, for all she cared. She stretched for the sake carafe and farted with the exertion. Let Omm take that in too. She stretched again, caught the carafe by the neck and tried to shake a last drop of rice wine into her goblet. But it was empty. She fell back depressed.

She placed her head sideways on the galley table among the empty dishes. Suddenly she felt lonely. The crew were all out there shagging, she knew. And here she was cooped up on zsf. She cried tears of self-pity. She heaved herself up from the table, left the Galley and wandered into the Pleasure Store. She felt much better when she came out except her fantasy had involved doing it with Lieutenant Sky which puzzled her since she'd never even remotely thought of the Lieutenant in a sexual way. There again stranger things had happened to her in the Pleasure Store. The chocolate fantasy was her favourite.

Mandella had the ship to herself and she continued to wander.

She passed the FunRoom, doubled back, went in, remembered Triple, dancing. Could she do it? There was no one but the ForceCode to see her. Her belly felt a bit stretched with the feast, but she put a track on and swayed to the music. It was a breezy Urthpop song, sung falsetto:

Diddly diddly ding dang doo
I slept with the stars
And I'll sleep with you
Bwoosh bwoosh, bwoosh bwoosh bwoosh!

Cuddly cuddly ding dang doh
Blow me a fire dream
And watch me go go go
Bwoosh bwoosh, bwoosh bwoosh bwoosh!

Diddly diddly ding dang doo
I slept with the stars

And I'll sleep with you
Bwoosh bwoosh, bwoosh bwoosh bwoosh!

She couldn't understand the lyrics but it was a light and breezy song and it had a easy rhythm that she could sway to. This was half aerobics, half dance. Despite her bloated feeling, she threw in a few steps to tilt the balance in favour of dance. Acid rushed up her throat. She swallowed hard. Put her hands on her knees and fought the nausea down.

She left the FunRoom to lie for a while in her sleepchamber.

Sleep came easily for once. And for the first half hour it was dreamless. When dreams came, she was always conscious of them being dreams, and fought to control them. But she didn't manage it. It was why she avoided sleep so much. But now she was tired and, all things considered, relaxed and happy. Her old fears were forgotten. And she dreamt and the dreams came and she fought to control what she dreamed, but couldn't because however the dreams began that dream always took over — she always lost control...

It was over in three seconds.

-MISSILES OFF! MISSILES OFF!
-VIS-ID NOT CONFIRMED AT 4-4 CAPTAIN! 3-4 ONLY!
-OVERRIDE! MISSILES OFF! (DNNNNK) WE ARE TARGET
LOCKED! AT DEEP SPACE SEVEN!
-ESCAPE VECTOR IMPOSSIBLE!
-EJECT! EJECT!
(BBHWOOOOSH!)

All it took was three seconds. Yet it had been three months in the making. She had replayed this scene so many times, in her dreams and awake.

-MISSILES OFF! MISSILES OFF!

One man, it was always clear, had had difficulty taking orders from a black woman. Especially orders of that magnitude. The trouble causing lieutenant was also the Gunner. Harry. A bald, flush-faced, obtuse manipulator, Harry had been around long enough to think he knew it all. He reckoned there was nothing he could learn from a rookie black Captain. And a woman at that. From Day One Mandella could tell he thought he, not she, should have been made Captain, and he went around telling the crew just that. She should have stamped on his first act of subordination, not calling her Captain when he first addressed her, but she'd let it go.

-VIS-ID NOT CONFIRMED AT 4-4 CAPTAIN! 3-4 ONLY!

Harry's voice. She looked. Their eyes clashed. His hand was cupped protectively over the missile firing icon. What in shit was he doing?

-VIS-ID NOT CONFIRMED AT 4-4 CAPTAIN! 3-4 ONLY!

Banshee Hunter H4. They were a rapidlaunch, dog-fighting ship. A hunter and interceptor. Assigned to protect the rear flanks of Command Fleet supply ships. There had been three months of nothing. She'd kept them drilled but they were battle rusty. They hadn't test-fired the missiles in all that time.

When an artificially propelled object was encountered, it could have been remote. That did not mean it could be identified at leisure. If it was hostile, space shrank. Lieutenant Harry triggered Banshee H4's recognition systems immediately. That much she had to credit him with. The systems went into overdrive. Four tests were run. Results of three tests confirmed in thousandths of a second they had a hostile craft in the vicinity. The fourth test stalled.

-VIS-ID NOT CONFIRMED AT 4-4 CAPTAIN! 3-4 ONLY!

She knew that! Why was Harry telling her that? Had he not taken in her Briefing? The Logos jamming systems could block the micro-trace-element test. She'd specifically remembered telling Officer Harry that. He'd been so busy playing mind-games with her he obviously hadn't absorbedmit.

3-4 ONLY!

There was obstinacy in his voice. A direct challenge to her. She might be captain of the ship, but he was the one calling the shots.

3-4 ONLY!

3-4 was no surprise. Entirely consistent with the briefing. There was no time to explain. Her look, brow plunged, mouth set in a scowl, had had to say it all. They had lost two seconds on that head to head. Two seconds they couldn't afford.

OVERRIDE!

Her voice blazed certainty.

MISSILES OFF!

She'd seen him hesitate then. Her own conviction destabilised his own. Now he raised that big fist of his. Flipped back the transparent, wide L shaped protective cover for the missile launch icon. He was blueing. She saw the blood drain from his face. The first time she'd seen that pink glow vanish. And the last. His finger never made it.

(DNNNNK)

The one sound all Captains were trained to Pavlovian standards on. The on-board personnel ejector silos opening. It worked simultaneously with the defence system Critical Five warning icon. It meant exactly what she'd called out:

WE ARE TARGET LOCKED! AT DEEP SPACE SEVEN!

The missiles were useless now. There were two options. Escape or eject. The answer came from the Navigator:

-ESCAPE VECTOR IMPOSSIBLE!

There was only one command after that:

-EJECT! EJECT!

She'd got out.

BBHWOOOOSH!

Cannoned into hyperspace in her individual life support capsule, in the split second before her first bout of unconsciousness, she'd seen Banshee Hunter 4 implode. No noise. Just a small red rosy glow at the base of the capsule. She drifted then, the oxygen feed keeping her alive. None of the others made it. She calculated she could survive ten bodyclock days before the dehydration killed her. Day Three to Day Ten would be the toughest. After Day Three there was no chance of being rescued. She had time to reflect in the capsule. Question herself. It had been Officer Harry's final mistake.

Could she have done it any differently?

By Day Two she was hallucinating. She saw black angels singing. Spirits with bodies whose every atom she could see. They were young. They soared with her, tumbling with her Capsule, following her as she span through this eternal night.

At the edge of Day Three moving into Day Four, she despaired. They were not coming. She turned down the oxygen supply so her consciousness could drift with the capsule to a blurred death. Could she have done it any differently?

Could she have done it any differently? The Debrief Panel had asked her that and she'd shrugged. She didn't think so. They needed to retrain or remove the bigots from the fleet. The Debrief Panel were all white. They didn't seem impressed. It would be cheaper in the long run, she'd said. Too many ships were being lost because of that kind of internecine strife on board. Cheaper. They'd looked up when she'd said that.

The precise sequence of events, dialogue and incidents leading up to the Banshee H4 disaster had been stored in Banshee H4's black box log. But that log had been vaporised with the rest of the ship. So they only had Captain Mandella's memory to go on, they explained. And they weren't satisfied with what she was telling them.

"Think hard, Mandella. We're all pilots together. What would you do differently, if you could rewind time?" they invited her.

It was a sucker question. She declined to offer them her head on a plate with some self-doubting, self-critical answer. If they wanted her head off, they would have to do the deed themselves.

Which they did.

The Unions hadn't supported her. The compensation package for the deceased crew multiplied by a factor of two if it was established that the captain had been negligent, and by a factor of three if she was found to have been reckless in her acts or omissions and if these acts or omissions were on balance the cause of the crew's death. The Unions had petitioned her to make something up, for the sake of the crew's dependents. But she declined to sacrifice her reputation on that particular altar. They had suspended her membership. That was bearable. She'd fought for and won the right to fly again. But not on a Hunter. On this Zsf engineering craft. Donkey ships.

-MISSILES OFF! MISSILES OFF!
-VIS-ID NOT CONFIRMED AT 4-4 CAPTAIN! 3-4 ONLY!
-OVERRIDE! MISSILES OFF! (DNNNNK) WE ARE TARGET
LOCKED! AT DEEP SPACE SEVEN!
-ESCAPE VECTOR IMPOSSIBLE!
-EJECT! EJECT!
(BBHWOOOOSH!)

Three seconds that explained her entire life. Could she have done it any differently? Three seconds. She had replayed this scene so many times in her dreams, turned it round this way and that, looking for nuances of nuances:

-MISSILES OFF! MISSILES OFF!

Mandella woke with a start. She was on zsf, not Banshee Hunter H4. Delivering oxygen, not missiles. Groggily, she drew herself up from her bed, stretched till her backbone and shoulder sockets protested. She could feel the skin on her belly stretched tight as could be, and remembered the meal. She breathed in deeply and stepped out of her sleepchamber.

Wisps of dreams dispersed even as she started walking, vague memories of relived fear, and by the time she reached the Bridge she had no idea what she'd been dreaming about.

The crew had forty five minutes to return. She brought up the trace monitor and saw three white blips against a red background, two of the blips almost on top of each other. She read it to mean that Officer Kaya was stuck like a burr to young Triple. So they should reach back on time. She felt the heaviness of the real food she'd had. She'd taken it without any anti-sickness powder. She didn't like the chemical tang it added to naturalfood. Now she half regretted it. No matter. She sat in her chair at the dais, and worked up the flight co-ordinates. They had a tight schedule and she wanted to be off Thuli and onto the next mission smartly.

"Come on then youth! Throw the punch! Then you'll see these bones jump on top of yuh!"

"Don't call me chupid!"

"So, what you call someone who go into a whorehouse wid no means of payment — King Solomon?"

Triple caught him then. A fast right cross that smacked into Kaya's lower lip. The young gunner went wild with excitement, hopping about, mouthing expletives at the older man, his fists raised and boxing the air.

"An I thought all that sex would a calmed you down," said Kaya, merrily pushing himself up off the floor. He dusted down his clothes, spat on and polished his right fist, and walked forward purposely.

Triple met him.

"Take this! Limpdick! And this!"

Three punches flew in from the youth. But Kaya, showing his old ringcraft skills, slipped them all. He was in close now. He took Triple by the waist in a bearhug, yanked him off his big feet and threw him over. They fell to the ground in a heap. Arms, legs, fists, elbows and feet flew about.

One of the huge Thulian Greeters pulled them apart.

"Either of you going to pay?" he said. "Or do we transportize you both?"

Transportization, whatever it was, didn't sound good to Kaya. He shook himself free. "All right, all right!" From inside his upper tunic pocket Kaya pulled out a small, square plastic wallet, containing one foil wrapped, genuine original cannabis seed. Gold dust on any planet.

He handed the wallet to the Greeter still crowding his personal space.

"Check it." Then he shot a glance at Triple. "You screw, I pay. It ain't right."

"I'll see you right, Pops," grinned Triple.

One Seven, who had been gone on an errand, turned up with the pod again.

"Everything OK?" she asked, taking in the scene.

"Yeah. Me and the boys're just hangin," said Triple, managing a grin though he was still flat on his back where he'd been dumped by Kaya.

Meanwhile, the Greeters had unfolded the foil and were looking over the seed. They had that 'hightimes' smile on their faces Kaya had seen so many times before. Cannabis seed was the gold standard of the Universe.

"You can go," one of the Greeters waved the humans away without looking up.

"Been nice knowing you," Kaya said sarcastically. He yanked Triple up to his feet: "Perhaps the young Prince would care to return to the ship with me, if he has finished getting himself laid?"

"With pleasure."

They got in the pod.

Hey, Bones?"

"Huh?"

"Sorry about the lip."

"Cha. You're too lippy by far."

I mean your bottom lip — it's bleeding."

Kaya ran a finger along the split, and grimaced. "Great. Split to raas."

Captain Mandella looked around the Bridge. Everyone was strapped in ready for take-off. Officer Kaya had a badly swollen lip. She hadn't asked how and he wasn't saying, which suited her fine. Officer Triple had this permanent sheepish grin on his face, so she guessed he'd got laid. Lieutenant Sky looked preoccupied. She had probably made an error of etiquette with the Thulians misfolded a napkin or something. She would find out what, and put the lieutenant's mind at rest. Mandella was sure none had noticed how queasy she herself was feeling.

Thuli's gravity was weak, and therefore she was playing it strictly by the book. She looked over her dais instrument array and read off the dial and strip readings to Officer Kaya:

"Oil pressure?"

"Oil pressure normal, Captain," replied Officer Kaya.

"Oil temperature?"

"Oil temperature normal, Captain."

"Engine air filters?"

"Filters clear, captain."

"Torque motors?"

"Torque motors normal, Captain."

Waking and waggling all zsf's flight critical components, Mandella satisfied herself everything was sound. All the main engine parameters were normal. All core systems feedback was confirmed operational. They were ready. Lieutenant Sky informed the air traffic control tower. The floodlights snapped off and, momentarily, there was darkness outside. The runway edge, centreline and exit lights came up.

"We have clearance for lift-off, Captain," said Lieutenant Sky.

Now the Thuli cargo had been delivered they needed only four of the main engines. The four engines had been preselected. "Ignite all Four," she commanded Officer Kaya.

"Igniting Four, Captain."

There was a quiet rumble of engine sound as the rocket engines fired.

"Down heat shields."

"Heat shields down, Captain."

"Engage drive."

Mandella took zsf forward onto the middle of the runway strip. The motion made her feel queasy again. Her forehead was clammy. She bit back bile. Officer Kaya let out the thrust slowly and the craft picked up speed along the runway, accelerating to two gravities.

"Passing liftoff velocity, Captain... Liftoff plus five... Plus ten—"

"Effect liftoff."

The zsf nose butted into the air, and zsf was airborne.

"Angle of ascent thirty degrees, twenty five."

"Undercarriage still out, Captain," interjected Officer Kaya.

"Undercarriage up," she called promptly, flicking the undercarriage lock switch.

Officer Kaya raised the undercarriage.

They climbed steadily.

At one kilometre, zero five, an alarm hooter went off. On both the rocket technician's and the captain's instrument arrays, the same icon flashed.

"Air filter blown on Engine Three. Engine on fire, Captain!" said Kaya.

"Shut down Three!" Mandella said reflexively. Her head span.

"Three shut down... Auto-extinguish effective." Officer

Kaya waited, expecting the next order. It didn't come. "We need more thrust, Captain. We're close to critical stall... Captain?"

Captain Mandella was slumped over the dais controls.

"Lieutenant, we have an emergency here. We need more thrust," said Kaya.

"Take over, Kaya," Sky said immediately.

Easier said than done. He had to switch over the Captain's Override first. Kaya unstrapped himself and crawled over to the Captain's dais.

The Captain was inert. She'd puked over the instrument array. He pulled her up off the dais controls and looked through the slime. The layout was not the same as his own. It was cluttered. A host of novel dials and strip instruments. Adjacent and identical knobs controlled vastly different systems and autopilot functions.

He found Engines by Probe Controls. He could feel the ship juddering to a Stall. He chose Five and Twelve simultaneously to offset the unequal starboard Thrust. Five failed to ignite. Twelve fired, but Two cut out. He hit Six, Seven, Twelve. The nose had dipped.

The remaining engines whined.

"Lick! Lick!" he cursed.

The on-board ambience lights began to flash. The Prepare To Eject code flashed.

Neither of the other two spoke. They knew the moment was ultracritical.

Kaya found fuel pressure. Turbo'd it. Six and seven came good. There was a lurch to starboard. Then Twelve came good too. There was a correcting lurch to port. The velocity slide peaked out. They began to climb sharply. Officer Kaya accelerated them to five gravities. He had not liked going up with just four engines anyway. It seemed unnecessarily parsimonious.

As they reached one kilometre five he felt weightlessness beginning.

"We're approaching zero g," he called. "Activating magnogravity." He braced himself as the ship's false gravity kicked in. "Surface gravity indicator at zero. Throttling back all engines." He looked around to the other two. "Relax. We've achieved orbit."

"*Majitu*, Kaya!" cried Triple.

"Yes, well done," said Lieutenant Sky. "Is the engine situation stable?"

"The fire's out in Three. I've shut down Five and Two as a precaution. The rest are on minimum burn, Lieutenant," said Kaya.

With captain Mandella incapacitated, command of the ship fell to Lieutenant Sky. She was aware that the Captain needed her medical attention, but knew the integrity of the ship was a priority. "There's no danger of supervening problems, Kaya?"

"I couldn't say that categorically. Until I've inspected the engines and found out what went wrong, there's no way of saying."

"All right. Postpone docking until you've found the problem and fixed it."

"If it can be fixed."

"Of course. Do that now," she said. She called to Officer Triple. "Come over here and help me with Mandella!"

"Yes, Lieutenant."

Kaya traced the problem back to the air filters on Three. The main grid and the ducting had been made from parts cannibalised from something else, an abandoned space station or reclaimed satellite he guessed, and were simply not up to specification, being already pocked with metal fatigue. When the Thuli dust had hit the filters, they'd clogged, then blown. That had caused the engine to overheat, and the fire. Learning from Three, engines Two and Twelve had self-blown fuses to prevent a repeat and a resulting fireball effect.

Presently Triple joined him. The two of them spent the best part of three hours ripping out all the pocked, brittle metalwork. Then it was down to Supplies to find fresh, solid plate, and riveting it into place. Then cleaning out Three engine. They worked hard and in silence, Kaya muttering one word directions to Triple. They fixed Three filter.

They did a systematic check on all eight filters. Five of the eight were Frankensteins and substandard. This would take another maybe eight hours. Kaya radioed to Lieutenant Sky with the bad news.

"I'm easy on that one, Kaya. The schedule's not so important," she said.

"Mandella wouldn't say that."

"Perhaps not. But I've got to do what I feel is right.

"You're the boss."

He sounded prickly. "Let's ensure the filters are all in prime condition before we restart the engines," the lieutenant suggested.

"I'll try... How's the captain?"

"She's on the up."

"What's her problem?"

"It doesn't look anything serious. Maybe duodenal lactic flux."

"All right. I'll repair the engines, you repair the Captain, Lieutenant."

"I'll do my best, Officer Kaya," Sky radioed.

"Ditto." The two worked on steadily and Kaya was impressed that Triple never once complained. Although the sixteen hours shift was long, it was bearable. You needed less sleep in space than on planets Besides, exercise was good for you. It prevented the muscle wastage that all long-tour astronauts were prone to. With thoughts such as these Officer Kaya comforted himself, as the two of them stripped the old filters.

Captain Mandella lay in the darkness under the foil blanket on the white cotton mattress of the softly vibrating bed. The Captain's condition was giving Lieutenant Sky cause for worry. She had pumped her stomach and given her a sickness inhibitor but the biodata showed little improvement and the stress readings were still high. The patient had a fever, and looked drawn. Her eyes were extremely light averse. That said, Sky was confident it was strep' food poisoning and she could deal with it. She was already reactivating an antibiotic for injection.

What concerned her more were the garrulous delusions. Mandella seemed to be dipping in and out of some kind of mindfunk. Her face became taut with fear, her body tense. The monitor showed the blood pressure level surge just before each bout. She got the signal that another one was on its way and put down the antibiotics flask.

Sky stroked Mandella's hand as Mandella rambled in fear:

"...trapped in this stick, this ick, this icky, stuck... stretched space-time web, some jester-god's fly, bug eye — stuck on a thread in this incessant whirl of stars, galaxies... time..."

"It's OK," soothed Sky, "you're safe here with us."

"Ploughing, plunging through plummeting down down! Down! The sharked sea of silent space—"

"It's OK. I'm here with you. Just hold onto me. I won't leave you. I'm here for you."

"Alone, cast off, remote—"

"You have us three—"

"Fate. The stars. Only the angels to save me."

"What angels, 'Della?"

"Black angels. The black angels — singing."

"What do they sing?"

"Promises, purpose, something other than perseverance. They are singing — can you hear them? They are singing."

"You need rest."

"No, to keep on is the thing. Make noise. Commotion. Fill the void. Keep the whelming silence from me."

"Rest now."

"Sky, Sky, I made a mistake."

"We all make mistakes."

"The Hunter..."

"No-one's hunting us."

"Escape vector..."

"Officer Kaya brought the situation under control. We're all alive. Everything's all right."

"Black angels, singing strong…"

Mandella's eyes were fevered. Lieutenant Sky administered an analgesic, a mild sedative, then the antibiotics. The contours of Mandella's face relaxed. The eyes closed. Sky slipped on the mask. She waited till Mandella drifted off to a high oxygen, deep, dreamfree sleep, then slipped out of the bay.

Sleep was the last thing on Kaya's mind, even though they had just finished test-firing the rockets. Everything was in order. The filters worked smoothly, even at max.

"Not bad," said Triple watching in the engine room.

"Not bad? A bumbaclaat miracle!"

They high-fived. "Right youth, now we haffi dock." They packed and stored the tools and reported back to the Bridge.

The cargo was in an equatorial orbit of Thuli. Although it was speeding round at sixty thousand kilometres per second, relative to each other, the two crafts were stationary. Docking was therefore, a low critical operation. He and Triple could do it, no problem. Mandella would approve. He was sure of that, what with the amount of time lost already.

Having mulled it over, Lieutenant Sky gave him the go-ahead.

Kaya used the twelve steering jets. Of the nineteen, these were the puniest, but also the most agile. Nevertheless, Kaya erred on the side of caution and it took him sixteen minutes to manoeuvre zsf so that its butt was aligned with the nose of the lead cargo train. Triple was in the Gunner's eyrie, supplying naked eye reconnaissance:

"Just tickle it two degrees to port… All right, hold!" Triple commsed.

"Continue reverse?" called Kaya.

"No, pitch up five."

"Five pitched," Kaya confirmed.

"Damp propulsion nozzles."

"Nozzles damped."

"All right, fade up docking tackle."

Kaya pushed Start Docking and on the outboard docking monitor, he saw the docking apparatus slowly protrude.

"Hold it," came Triple, "Kiss Left Seven to Starboard point seven."

Officer Kaya made the adjustment.

"All set. Hitch the train!" said Triple.

Kaya tweaked up the retro jets.

"Train hitched?" called Kaya. He couldn't see clearly on the monitor. Thuli's atmospheric dust had clouded the lens.

"Kiss aft to port a millimetre... OK. You got it — do you hear wedding bells?" called Triple.

Sure enough, a tone played on at the dais to indicate docking was complete. The dais's cargo instruments loaded data. The four remaining carriages — two water, one cobalt, one oxygen — were all full and intact.

"All right, Lieutenant Sky. I think we're ready to rocket," Kaya said proudly.

"Not a regulation docking. But competent all the same!"

"Wha?" Kaya looked up. Captain Mandella had appeared at the Bridge doors.

"Stand down now, Kaya, I'll take over."

Kaya willingly stood down. "You feelin' all right, Captain?"

"Cosmic," Mandella confirmed.

She didn't look it, Sky thought. She looked drawn. The last biodata Sky had seen suggested another two hours recovery time at least before clearthink. But Mandella had that stubborn, don't-you-question-my-authority look in her eye, and the Lieutenant kept schtum. So did the others.

Mandella assumed the dais, took her chair. She looked at the on-screen engine diagnostic reports with satisfaction. They had full power. "Crew, take your seats — Officer Triple get down from the Gunnery. Harness up and place seat settings on maximum g-force resistance. We're going for hyperburn!"

Mandella still has raised temperature and a high strep count, but she is improving rapidly. I told her about her early bout of delirium. Mentioned key words — her feeling of being hunted, that she was all alone apart from the angels. I suggested sometimes the truth comes in such fevers. Would she like to talk her fears over? She was her usual reticent self in response. She said one day she'd explain, but now wasn't the time. I asked her why she had overeaten:

"Is it a self-image problem? Or an overcompensation for being so controlled a personality?"

"I was just sick, Sky," she replied, "I grossed out. I puked up. Simple. Cause and effect. That yukky rice wine was company issue. I should have known it'd be off."

She switched the subject by asking me about Thuli — what had I got up to there — had I got laid? I confessed yes, I had had sex with a Thulian. The news upset her:

"You of all people!"

"I'm sorry."

"The ForceCode counsels restraint. There are myriad — you understand? — myriad dangers, Lieutenant!"

After a brief, cynical enquiry about the mechanics of fucking on low gravity planets, the Captain moved through various negative outcome scenarios. Her worse case was that they had implanted something in me. I assured her I had scanned myself and I was clear. She was not impressed, and said something about the entire crew running around fornicating while she was stuck on zsf. This opinion was surprising since we'd agreed that she'd stay on board to get some rest. It was her idea. In view of her mood and her health, I chose not to alarm her further. My having had sex with a Kieran had hurt her. To go on and say that Kieran Five Five was not human would have been too much.

PS. Overheard:

"Triple: I wanna be like you, Bones — balanced and calm, and slow."

"Kaya: Less of the slow, please!"

From Sky's Private Log.

Why do I punish myself for lying to Mandella? Does she really need to know I had sex with an alien, and not just a Thulian? To save someone from pain, lies are sometimes necessary. Moreover, has she been transparently honest with me? My sex life is none of her business. I don't think she likes sex. The very idea seems to repel her.

I hide this secret from Mandella. It is better this way. We all wear masks: dissemble. The lover, the loser, the jailer, the fool, the liar. The number and dance of our masks is our personality. What if we removed them — became transparent in soul, like true angels?

We cannot know each other entirely. The most we can truly know of others is their aura — their soulglow. This aura can only be seen by those capable of deep meditation. It is a rare sensibility. (That is not a boast.)

Aura seers have often been considered Intuitives, Psychics. Yet if we are willing to let go of the ego and its selfish dreams, personal ambition, lusts, hates, loves and other outer desires, we can all be seers. Transcending ego, we can experience the soulglow. Only selfishness blinds the eyes to the soul...

Mandella has kept the rockets on hyperburn to make up for lost time. It will still be three weeks shiptime before we have traversed this Galaxy. It seems young Triple had a good shore leave. There is a joyous bounce in his step. I overheard him breezing with Kaya:

Kaya: What's that picture you carryin', youth?

Triple: Kieran Three Eight.

Kaya: Give it here. Looks like any other Kieran to me.

Triple: She's my girl — she and One Nine.

Kaya: There's another girl too?

Triple: On Thuli, two is a lonely number!

Kaya: You made it with both of them, right?

Triple: At the same time — Had them screaming with pleasure!

Kaya: Well, you had them laughing for true.

Triple: Don't be jealous, Bones... So much better than the Pleasure store. I'll never use that thing again.

Kaya: (Chuckles) We'll see, Studs. It's a long way to the next planet.

Triple: Girl on every planet at this rate. It's my charisma.

Kaya: (Aside) And my ganja.

PS: I have taken to composing poems as an extra form of meditation. Are they good or bad? I don't know. Let posterity judge them.

Three days hyperburn gained them back the lost time and Captain Mandella was satisfied. She ordered a return to cruise speed to conserve fuel and held course for Archaos and the next delivery. She took the time to read the crew's reports on Thuli. Not that they detained her long. Officer Kaya reported nothing that she had not known before. It was the same with Lieutenant Sky. She got the feeling neither of them could be bothered.

Mandella didn't reintroduce the Shift-to-Shift drills. There was no way she could, in fairness to them. Not after all they'd done. Officer Kaya had averted a disastrous stall in her absence. He and Triple had then shown a phenomenal work rate in repairing the damage to the blown Three filter and replacing all the others. Kaya had discovered they were flying a pile of spot-welded space junk. This fact was new to her — Command hadn't so much as hinted — but did not surprise her. There were no lengths Command wouldn't go to in their economies, she surmised.

She had a grudging respect for Officer Kaya now. After

the low of Kayiga, his recent acts had evened things up in her estimation of him. Not that she told him. She liked a crew that stayed on its toes. Lieutenant Sky had pleased her too. She had been acting Captain for all of sixteen hours, and had done a good job. She'd done it her own way apparently, more consensual than commanding, which in the long run, Mandella and all time-served Captains knew, never worked; but she'd done it. A new confidence had surfaced in Sky's voice, her manner. And the two males had accepted this. Good for Sky. It bode well for the future, if she, Mandella should be incapacitated again.

★

The next shifts saw Mandella heal physically Her psyche though, was still troubled. It seemed now that Sky had had some intimation of this during her illness. The lieutenant had been zealous in offering her counselling sessions for her 'mind disturbance'. Mandella had declined, first politely and then rudely. Sky refused to let it drop. Mandella found Sky's solicitations irritating in the extreme.

Nevertheless it was Sky who maybe forced the nightmare loop to jump out of its groove. It had been the same old footage — Mandella dreaming the dream:

-MISSILES OFF! MISSILES OFF!
    -VIS-ID NOT CONFIRMED AT 4-4 CAPTAIN! 3-4 ONLY!
    -OVERRIDE! MISSILES OFF! (DNNNNK) WE ARE TARGET LOCKED! AT DEEP SPACE SEVEN!
    -ESCAPE VECTOR IMPOSSIBLE!
    -EJECT! EJECT!
    (BBHWOOOOSH!)

She woke to find the Lieutenant in her sleep chamber, kneeling beside her, stroking her forehead.

"Mandella, you've been dreaming again!" Sky said later her eyes had been staring ahead. Her teeth had been so clenched the muscles of her cheeks twitched.

"What's the matter? What do you see?"

"The Hunter. The Hunter. But it's too late."

"What's too late? Who's hunting? Listen to me 'Della! You can't keep tormenting yourself. Tell me what you see. Tell me now."

But Mandella woke then, from the postdream trance. Her eyes were clouded with fear. She looked Sky over slowly. "I don't know, Lieutenant. What I see. Wisps. Angels. Fragments... What are you doing here?"

"I hate to see you like this. Next time you dream, turn and confront your pursuer. Stand your ground. Challenge. It's the only way to end your nightmare. I promise."

Of course, the Lieutenant's advice had been based on a fundamental misunderstanding. The Hunter was not an image or metaphor, it was her last ship, Mandella knew. But the lieutenant had meant well. And maybe, subconsciously, Sky's words had some effect on her.

Mandella's tactic, once she realised the attention her sleep shift was attracting, was to control the nightmare by controlling entry into dreamstate. On her daily, three hour sleepshifts she began to option full-shift fathom-sleep. It meant taking a hypnotic, but it was worth it. Fathom-sleep was dreamless.

But in the back of her mind, she knew the nightmare was trying to tell her something. That it would not let her go until she understood. And that she had to resolve it.

She came off fathom-sleep whenever she felt strong enough.

The first time she came off and dreamt again, there was a development. She still dreamt of Banshee H4. But spliced into the disaster reels and projected onto the screen of her dream memory for the first time was a moment of humour. How Harry had once cracked a joke just after they'd left for the tour. She'd laughed. The whole Banshee Hunter 4 crew had laughed. It was something about the correct way to greet an accountant. In itself the joke was nothing. But that she had recalled it at all was totally unexpected for her. The first time for her a happy memory of Banshee had surfaced.

Encouraged, she stayed off the fathom-sleep.

That was tempting fate.

Next time, the full nightmare came snorting into her dreamstate. First an apocalyptic, riderless horse, rearing high, stenching of fear. Mandella was petrified, but determined. She would tame the horse. See the dream through. The horse whinnied off. And the dream recurred. This time at twice the usual speed:

MISSILES OFF! MISSILES OFF!/

VIS-ID NOT CONFIRMED AT 4-4 CAPTAIN! 3-4 ONLY!/

OVERRIDE! MISSILES OFF! (DNNNNK) WE ARE TARGET LOCKED!/

AT DEEP SPACE SEVEN!/

-ESCAPE VECTOR IMPOSSIBLE!/

-EJECT! EJECT!/

(BBHWOOOOSH!)

Now new factums stood out: *Escape Velocity Impossible!* The Navigator had been fast with it. In the time he had taken to say those words he could have ejected, saved himself. She had never considered that before. The navigator's self-sacrifice.

Another new factum. *Deep Space Seven!* That was unbelievable. The first time she'd heard it in her dreams. She must have blocked it. The intruder had been at two o'clock. *Deep Space Seven* meant the threat was at seven o'clock. Only now, in her dream, did she realise. *Two* intruders had been present, not one.

The first, the one they'd successfully identified, was a drone, a decoy. The second, the one they'd missed until too late, was the real thing.

Simple really. She'd been outwitted. She should have done a global awareness trace immediately she spotted the first. It would have shown up the other craft at Deep Seven — the craft that had shot them down. *Lieutenant Harry had been right all along.*

It was no longer fear, but realisation. The fear had been of this knowledge. The awful knowledge of her mistake. The riderless horse retreated. Instead of terror, came tears.

She woke from her dreamsleep soaking wet, chastened, remembering everything.

Sky hadn't been there. She was glad of that. Her shame was private.

For forty-eight hours after the dream, Mandela didn't eat. She explained to Sky it was the aftermath of the food poisoning and she was still taking liquids. Sky hung around trying to get inside her head, but Mandella colded her.

Gradually, tentatively, Mandella went back to the memory, as if to clean a wound She would be her own doctor. She realised now, why Human Factors Unit had been sitting in on her debrief. Command would have had data on the twin craft presence in Banshee Hunter 4's zone. In the debrief, she had shown total unawareness of that second Logos craft. That was why she'd been sidelined. Not for failing. But for not properly analysing her failure. So be it, Mandella thought. No use petitioning them now. Far too late to appeal.

She was reconciled now. She slept and the reel never played. It was gone, pushed out from her subconscious to her conscious mind. Captain Mandella began eating again. She kept herself occupied with the send-only briefings from Command which described the Zimbabwe Space Force's wider activities, and generally was civil if a little more distant than usual.

Meanwhile, the crew worked efficiently and harmoniously. Kaya had his quiet days. Triple had his sulky, grumpy days. Sky had her meditative days. But there were no major problems. Zsf-e5 journeyed on.

In the deep backwaters of NilSol West, you were all alone. In this unmapped zone of no suns, no water, no oxygen, there was no life, nor any possibility of life. It was the furthest known hinterland, the coldest, loneliest frontier. Captain Mandella thrust her hand into her tunic trouser pocket. Her index and middle fingers slowly rubbed the worn velvet swatch. She had a vague feeling of unease. She tried to cure it by going through the spacesam log but this merely unsettled her more. They had just left Hilda's Yard. It had been a nightmare to navigate. Its constant low level gravitational field attracted all the unanchored, heavyweight debris of space and it had become a museum of space folly: elaborate unfinished structures, huge shelved projects, gigantic abandoned visions, monumental half-built dreams. Just scrolling through the Hilda log was depressing. Multiple lifetimes of endeavour reduced to so much junk. Dutifully, she had ticked off all the structures they'd passed. Looking at the log again served no effective purpose. It was NilSol they had to deal with now.

NilSol posed a different set of problems. It was barren. So barren all zsf-e5's sensors had flashed up error codes the moment they entered. The sensors had never encountered so much nothing. At least this was how Officer Triple had explained it when she'd asked. But he'd conceded that the ForceCode, of which the sensors were an extension, had become increasingly erratic of late: false readings, bizarre routeing plans, erroneous maintenance chits and even new menu suggestions had been made. Captain Mandella reset the sensors and they functioned normally. She had been having to override the ForceCode more and more. When it had started suggesting personality improvement exercises for each of the crew, Officer Kaya had joked that the ForceCode was beginning to think it was human.

Against this background, it was entirely understandable that Captain Mandella responded with a degree of uncertainty to the sensor strip reading Officer Triple brought to her attention.

"What does it mean?" she commsed him. It was Officer Triple's job to explain the cursed instrument readings he watched over, not just flag them up.

"That there's something out there," Officer Triple said.

"Yonder?"

"That's it."

"At least the sensor says so," she said doubtfully. "Which array?"

"Vurt-radar."

"That one's tripped before," Mandella said. "Reset it and see."

Officer Triple did as asked. He was back to her promptly. "I think we have a situation here. The reading's back up."

She took Triple's warning seriously.

"Everyone strap in. We may have a UDO." Her own money was still on it being software glitch, but she gave a second burst of precautionary commands. "Officer Kaya, lower shields. Place rockets on standby. Officer Triple, take up at Gunnery. Lieutenant Sky prepare comms." Even as she spoke, Mandella herself was running a global reconnaissance check. She was not going to be suckered by another Logos drone.

Nothing showed on 'global' but the object Triple had already identified. Summoned by the alarm, Officer Kaya stumbled through the doors. He'd been in the mess and had brought the plastic tray of food with him. He was still shovelling food into his mouth with his hands.

Slack, Mandella thought. Emergency procedure was to abandon. Not grab your dinner and then run. Priorities, she cooled herself. Later, she'd reprimand. Not now.

"Officer Kaya, are shields lowered?"

"Lowering shields now Captain." He took his seat on the Bridge.

"Triple," she commsed, "What's the dump on that UDO?"

All she had was a little blue dot on her screen. Magnified, it became a blurred blue hemisphere. A blur magnified was still a blur. She needed the dump. Her mind hopped possibilities. Asteroid. Spacejunk. Missile. Mine. Craft. Fleet of crafts. Or nothing. They needed to know which and fast. She, more than anyone, knew that.

"Officer Kaya, unhitch cargo!"

"Cargo unhitched Captain."

She felt the kick of speed as they left the ponderous bulk train behind them.

"Eject strafe then elevate at five g. to DS Plus four. Then jitterbug."

"Strafe ejected. Elevating, captain."

Zsf-e5 lurched upwards in execution of the avoidance routine. In the place where the craft had been were millions of heat charged, centimetre square metal and glass sheets, in a formation that was an an exact replica shape of zsf-e5. From any great distance, the chaff would be mistaken for zsf-e5.

The avoidance action routine completed, and jitterbug action came on.

"How do you see it, Kaya?" Mandella asked, stumped herself.

"Just one more piece of junk heading for Hilda's." Kaya replied.

"Impossible," said Mandella. "This is NilSol."

The repulsive anti-gravity of NilSol meant the object could never have merely drifted into the zone. It either had power or had been propelled. They needed data. The problem was to catch more data they would have to put out signals. Those signals could be detected and from them the ship identified and attacked.

"Nothing showing," called Triple from the Gunnery. "We need signal boost."

"Launch comms buoy!" Mandella ordered.

"Comms buoy launched." replied Kaya.

"It's probably nothing," said Lieutenant Sky.

"Get on comms." snapped Mandella.

The comms buoy began sending to and receiving signal echoes from the object, relaying the information to zsf-e5.

The buoy data came streaming in. Officer Kaya scanned the object verification data coming through the comms buoy strips: "Proceeding West South West... Propulsion is at 0.3 velocities, vectoring is 0.2. Mass is five Newtons. There is soft rotation, clockwise. Independent propulsion check is either negative or noise—"

"Which?" rapped Mandella. There was a world of difference.

"The sensors are unsure. There's no heat plume suggesting rockets. But there appears to be a chill plume. That could mean there is a heat exchange at post-power and pre-exhaust, or it could mean that the craft itself is naturally cooler than the surrounding atmosphere. At this distance it's hard to tell. Can we edge closer, Captain?"

"This is no time for suck it and see. What is its badge?" Mandella said.

"Unbadged on micro, radar and visicheck, Captain." replied Kaya. This was unusual. "It's no asteroid," he added. "I'm getting more now. It's an artificial structure. Check this."

X-ray spectrometry was showing a deep hulled, riveted metal structure, twelve times zsf-e5's size. There was a nuclear reactor at the stern. The inner perimeter was a network of piping and ducts. At the nucleus of the structure, stacked six high, were regular structures, each two and a half metres long, a metre wide and a metre high.

They all looked it over on their screens.

"Honeycomb." said Sky, thinking aloud.

"Maybe a hotel, a floating hotel." said Kaya.

Mandella thought weaponry. The regular cells could be

missile silos. She saw no virtue in lingering.

Suddenly the X-Ray boom sensors blanked. They could no longer see the UDO's interior.

"What happened there?"

"I don't know, Captain." It was Triple.

She wasn't going to hang around. "Officer Kaya, scoop buoy, hitch cargo! Then prepare rockets for hyperburn."

"Yes, Captain. Preparing—"

"Wait!"

It was Sky.

"What now Sky?" Mandella cut in.

"There's a beacon pulse." Sky said.

"Hold engines!" Mandella looked over the buoy readings again. One radar scan was tripping back and forth 49 then 50, 49 then 50. There could be any number of explanations for the fluctuation. Instrument malfunction. Software failure. NilSol's anti-gravity creating blur. Still it was an imperative of Command Control Protocol that all emergency beacons be logged and checked out. And from the look of her, Mandella's jut-jawed Lieutenant was holding her it.

"It is a beacon, Captain," Officer Kaya called. He tweaked the signal up so it came through loud and clear. It was a standard being-in-distress call.

Captain Mandella eyeballed her second-in-command. "Lieutenant Sky, have you had Meal Two yet?"

"What's that got to do with it, Captain?"

What it had to do with it was if the lieutenant got off her Bridge, she, the Captain would be able to fly this damn ship as best served the interests of the crew instead of imperilling them on some wild beacon-check. Lieutenant Sky was looking back at her all stiff necked and haughty from the moral high ground. Moral or not, high ground was where you got shot at. But there was nothing for it. Mandella sniffed a response:

"Nothing, Lieutenant. Just a thought."

"Should I acknowledge the signal then?" It was the approved procedure.

122

"Yes, you do that, Lieutenant."said Mandella. She looked back down at her instrument array. Most people avoided trouble. The Lieutenant sought it out.

"What next Captain?" asked Kaya.

"Approach with caution, all shields down." Mandella said. Then she commsed Officer Triple in the Gunnery. "Officer Triple, remove safetys from the laser. I'm handing you roll controls. If you see anything at all suspicious, don't hesitate."

"Yes, Captain."

Triple was strapped tightly into the single bucket seat of the Gunnery. He popped a gelatine stick into his mouth and chewed. One hand held the craft joy stick, the other hovered over the range of offensive and defensive weaponry options. His head was encased in the slim black panvision target select and destroy headgear. His eyes scanned the panvision. He was nervous, but not overly so. He had his training to fall back on. All those Cadet Ship rehearsals. All the seminars and tests. Then there were the drills the captain had put him through. OK, he had a peashooter of a laser. But if used smartly, it could do as much damage as something vastly bigger, he positived. You make do: Positive Mental Attitude.

Triple kept his eyes on the headscreen. Bones was taking them in on a slow zig-zag towards the blip. In reaction speed critical situations, he, Triple, was always going to be the one to get them out of trouble. A lot was riding on him getting it right. He'd heard the talk of the captain's past. How she'd lost her last ship in dubious circumstances. He didn't have an opinion on it because he didn't have the facts. He only knew that, at this level, a hair's breadth separated success from failure.

As the zsf sensors got closer the object's profile came up in detail on Triple's headgear. He didn't recognise the shape at all. A membrane-less hull the shape of two soup bowls, one lidding the other. All of it a low conspicuity, matt black colour. The deck was flat and almost featureless. He surfed Recogs. It was not any known hostile structure. It had no

123

recognisable weapons system. The propulsion system was identifiable as nuclear. But it gave off no detectable gases. It wasn't built for flight. Its double soupbowl shape defied all flight profiling laws.

Triple kept scrutinising as zsf circled. It looked more a station than a craft. Yet it was too small for a station. It had a high density hull. He was looking for a weak spot on it. He knew if he fired, and the hull was armoured and the laser failed to impact, their position would be known and retaliation could be expected if there was any being on board. He had to assume that. So he might have one shot. Then they'd have to shift position fast. Shoot 'n' roll, the manoeuvre was called.

"Any idea, Captain?" Lieutenant Sky asked, from the Bridge.

"Hush," replied Mandella.

Alarm lights had came on. Icons flashed on the dais instrument array. Mandella felt adrenaline dripping into her gut.

Quickly she checked the icons. The scintillation counter and atmospheric probe both had positive recognition feedback. Both counter and probe agreed. It was a Logos sourced craft.

Radar came in with the same conclusion. That made code 3/4: enemy craft. Logos. The blood pulsed loud in her ear. The only reason they hadn't gone 4/4 was the absence of any detectable weaponry. Instead this infernal distress beacon.

Mandella commsed Officer Triple quietly. "Set target!"

"Target set, Captain." Triple came back.

"Zig forty, twenty, forty, through 360, North to West!"

As zsf span and zigged to make itself missile-elusive, Mandella scanned the reconnaissance strips again. She wouldn't be caught twice by the Logos decoy move. They all reported zero other presences. It was just the UDO and themselves.

"Target lock!" Mandella ordered.

"Target locked, Captain," said Triple.

They were within protocol to explode the craft there and then, distress beacon or no. It was a Logos craft after all. But Mandella held off.

"Triple, lift signals jam. Lieutenant Sky, open comms."

"Signal jam lifted."

"Comms open, Captain."

She was giving the craft one last chance.

"This is zsf. Distress signal registered. Any soul there?" The crew were silent as Sky relayed the message in analogue and digital.

Most beacons had a second stage response code for answering rescuer's "Responding-To-Beacon" signals.

Sky had radio and vidcoms channels open and live. Any signal at all from the hulk would be picked up.

But there was no response. Calmly, Captain Mandella moved to stage two:

"Test fire laser!"

A strobe of light that flashed from the cockpit past the bows of the craft, and on into the depths of NilSol's infinitesimal beyond. It lasted a moment. Though the afterglow stayed briefly in the Bridge crew's eyes.

Mandella blinked. "This is the captain of zsf-e5, responding to beacon emergency signal West South West NilSol UFO. Acknowledge. Acknowledge."

Still no response.

She had done her duty. The set protocol was exhausted. She commsed the Gunnery. The beaconed UDO was a maritime hazard."Officer Triple, vaporise craft!"

Suddenly the airwaves woke:

"Wait! Wait! Wait!"

"Stand fire!" Mandella shouted.

"We've got something!" said Sky redundantly. "Analogue short wave 296.5!"

"Wait! Wait! Wait!"

It was a pleading and angry, male human voice. Mandella tensed. What were they about to get involved in?

"This is Captain Mandella of Zimbabwe Space Force-e5. Who are you and what is your problem?"

"Coming through on short vid now." Sky murmured.

The Bridge's forward-facing membrane fuzzed then filled with a grainy, crudely flickering, picture. It could have been anything. Simultaneously, the same voice that had shouted the plea, came over zsf's PA, deep and embittered.

"I am Commander Idris of Logos Ramjet Fleet Four. Sole survivor of this prison ship."

Who would anchor a prison ship in NilSol of all places? Mandella spoke warily.

"I am Captain Mandella of Zimbabwe Space Force Engineering Five. "You are a Logos ship?" she quizzed.

There was a pause, before the voice answered.

"Yes. But I am an enemy of Logos. We were all enemies of the…" the voice trailed off, bitter and seemingly exhausted from the very effort of talking. "Save me," it murmured, "it is your duty to save me!"

The screen was becoming clearer by the second and Mandella looked hard. The head and shoulders of a bald, smooth skinned, copper-coloured black man, in his late thirties appeared on the large screen membrane. He wore no shirt or vest, and his skin glistened with some glycerine insulant-like gel. The screen definition was good enough to see the raised bumps of goose pimples on his flesh. He had prominent eyes, a long, sloping jaw, a square, symmetrical face, even white teeth behind bowed lips (the upper a shade darker than the copper of the lower). He had no eyebrows or eyelashes, marbled brown irises, hard black pupils and a broad gaze. His face looked composed, and stern, his body tense with either pain or cold, or both. He was shaking slightly. The camera which was sending the pictures to zsf never altered its position or focus. It was a black man. She'd recognised it in the voice. The immediate logic of a position such as this was taken care of by the military truism, 'my enemy's enemy is my friend'. Captain Mandella, of course, didn't see it so simply. Why should she believe the man? She trusted nothing and no-one emanating from Logos. She ordered Triple to keep the hulk covered, and told Sky to switch on polygraph analysis. Then she asked, "What are the silos on board your ship for?"

"There are no silos."

"We've counted nine hundred."

"Those are cells. Prisoners are shelved there. This is a prison ship."

Plausible, Mandella thought, but no more than that.

"Please come soon," the figure continued, "I'm using my last power…" There was desperation in the voice, under the bitterness and anger.

Fools rush in where angels fear to tread. "Explain yourself, Commander Idris. What is the ship doing in NilSol? Why is it without markings?"

"Too many questions," the voice warned. "I don't have much power left. Come and get me. Then you'll have all the answers you want."

"I've got time," Mandella said. "I can't do anything without answers."

"This ship is a prison ship," the voice began, "and on board are the dead bodies of nine hundred Logosniks."

"Logosniks?"

"I will try to explain, but I'm not an experienced Describer," he said, "I have no oratory, I can only tell the facts, even though it seems, my life depends on it."

"Carry on," sniffed Captain Mandella, "you're doing fine so far."

"Our founding heroes were space pilots from Urth," Commander Idris began. "Half a millennium ago, they flew in a flotilla far beyond where anybody had dared explore before. They came across a Galaxy which had a sun and four sets of twin, life-sustaining planets. They named the Galaxy Logos and hoisted their own flag.

"Urth military authorities objected. Working for the military, they could only claim in the name of Urth's military, Urth's junta said. The pioneers refused to return, or to recognise Urth junta's authority. They refused to pay Urth Galaxy tributes. They were labelled renegades by Urth and the first war between Urth forces and Logos began. Urth got the worst of this and finally abandoned Logosians to their fate.

"With the war over, the period of building began. Logos founders had a vision: to kiss into being a bold new world. Raw materials were readily available in Logos. A breeding programme was devised. Soon a substantial population was established on all eight planets. New cities sprang up, new technologies were discovered, a brand new civilisation arose. The vision held strong. There was a new system of government, a new jazz of human souls. The spirit of hope reverberated from Logos throughout the Universe. But you know all this."

"Carry on," said Mandella grimly. She knew most of it. He had omitted small things like the slaughter of the native species by the Logos founders, but the story was on the whole accurate.

As Idris continued, Sky commsed Mandella. She was puzzled: "Polygraph readings are blank."

Mandella silently acknowledged the message. Officer Triple told her he had got a fix on the broadcast frequency, and had accordingly targeted what he took to be the cockpit, fifty metres below the docking sphere at the top centre of the hulk's deck.

Meanwhile, Commander Idris went on:

"A snowflake is uniquely beautiful until it dissolves. We had a wonderful society, until the ties of solidarity unravelled."

"How did that happen?" Mandella prompted. There were intelligence circulars of interplanetary warfare in Logos, but no firm details.

Idris shivered.

"It's the oldest story — the rise and fall of Empires beginning with Urth's African Songhay and continuing through the Romans."

"Tell it." said Mandella.

There was a moment's hesitancy, then Idris continued. "Fudoh the Immovable was elected to power. Gradually, rule by plebiscite became rule by dynasty. Why? Why ever? The seduction of power. The stupidity of the led—"

"He came to power?" Mandella started, trying to keep him tracked.

"Yes. Fudoh and his clan ruled by fear. The new Government was a race system, organised along blood lines. There were rebellions from the excluded clans on all planets. Fudoh mercilessly repressed them. In time, the old way was forgotten, and his tyranny was accepted. About this time he acquired the title, the Immovable.

"But I and a few others kept the dream of democracy alive. We read the teachings of Marcus Garvey, his prophets Robert Nesta Marley and Nelson Mandela, as well as the words of our founders. I talked to my people."

"Your people?"

"I was a general in the Logos defence force. Fleet commander of almost a thousand Ramjet jets. We controlled

129

the airspace around Xeres FourB. Most of my fleet's pilots were black — part of the Fudoh regime's segregationist thinking. His praetorian guard is all family and white. I approached my fleet pilots individually. One by one they came over to my way of thinking, understood the material, political and spiritual benefits of change. Time eventually came to move from theory to practise. To challenge Fudoh. The plan was to seize Xeres FourB, and so catalyse the latent discontent and ignite a Logos-wide rebellion. Logos itself had become an aggressive presence in the Universe. At war with many Galaxies, including Urth. We hoped Urth would come in and assist in Fudoh's overthrow."

"I remember rumours of internal dissent," Mandella confirmed. "But nothing came of them, did they?"

"No. My plan leaked — an informer. There was a trial. The verdict was a foregone conclusion. Fudoh could have executed us, but he was too cunning for that. Death would have created martyrs. Instead the sentence for all nine hundred was 'life beyond life'. We were placed in a deep-ice coma. Electronic-valved cyanide implants were embedded in our upper arms. Then we were loaded onto a prison ship — this prison ship-and towed into NilSol. There we were left to our living death."

"Still alive though, at that point?" Mandella pointed out.

"Yes. Food, oxygen and waste elimination system supports were attached venously to the right arm of all prisoners. But a valved, loaded drip was attached to the lower left arm. The drip's load was a cyanide reagent. At any time, Fudoh could order the drip valves opened by pulse from Logos. The reagent would activate the cyanide implant. So, although we were far away in NilSol, he had this power of life and death over us. More importantly, our people knew that. The people knew that to rebel would be to sentence us, their leaders in NilSol, to death."

The screen was still not wholly clear, but Mandella noticed lacerations on the hands, and tape patches on the upper arms, with dark encrustations that could be dried blood: she couldn't tell the exact colour because the screen colour was jumping. Behind Idris was what looked like a wall of controls that almost resembled some of zsf's. Before him was a steel table, on which he rested his arms. There were no acoustics but for the tinny transmission that was his voice.

"You say everyone except you on the ship is dead?" she said.

"Yes. Fudoh released the cyanide, I think. The power systems shut down. The life support and coma systems stopped. But I survived. I woke. I grabbed off the drips. I discovered the valve of the drip attached to my left arm — the one controlling the cyanide reagent — had failed to open. I ripped the drip out. Then I got out of my deep-ice tray, to find corpses on every cell shelf. It was then I realised I was the only survivor. My friends, my comrades in arms, are all dead."

"How long ago was this, that you woke?"

"Five oxygen canisters ago."

"Is there food on board?"

"I... I fed from the others. They would have wished it. With the cyanide, it amounts to poisoning myself. I can't do that anymore anyway. The corpses are beginning to rot. Maggots. Flies are present below. I can't keep them frozen, the corpses. I diverted what was left of the body support power cells to the cockpit for heat, light, and transmission power. There's a minimal supply left, even of that. Hardly enough, even to transmit to you."

So that was the story. It was neat. Well woven. And consistent. But was it fact or fiction? Was he lying? With the polygraph down, Mandella had no objective test. She was unsure.

"You say you commanded a fleet?"

The Logosian looked surprised to be questioned further, but answered promptly. "Yes, nine hundred and eighty five craft."

"What formation did it fly?" she pressed.

On the screen Mandella saw him slowly smile as he answered her:

"Strategic ambiguous. A chaos formation. Do you know it?"

She didn't.

"I'll ask the questions. You answer. What were the names of your wing commanders?"

"Hendricks and Roach," he said tetchily.

"What was your scramble take-off protocol acronym?"

"We didn't use one."

"How do you use a gimbal, Commander Idris?"

He mocked her.

"Gimbals are obsolete for Logos craft, Captain Mandella. Our technologies are far in advance of such a primitive device."

"That's not my impression."

"I don't mean to antagonise you, but those zsf battle crews with actual experience in the combat zones will confirm what I'm saying."

A scintilla of remembered fear cut into Mandella: *The Hunter fireball*. She blanked it quickly, pressed on with the cross-examination.

"What are meteorological conditions like on Xeres FourB?"

"Poor."

"Be precise."

"Nitrogen, free oxygen, water vapour, a strong ionosphere, screening Violet layer, surface pressure of sixty five millibars, ice crystal clouds, high wind velocity, two seasons... Enough?" Idris glowered haughtily on the screen. "I get the impression you're testing me, Captain Mandella."

It was said as an accusation. Mandella ignored him. "Why is the prison ship unbadged?"

"It is? I don't know. I imagine they thought if it were unbadged, you would be more likely to leave it alone. But your guess is as good as mine."

"The walls of your ship are impenetrable to x-ray and ultraviolet searches. Why is that?"

"As I was saying, Logos technology—"

"On a mere prison ship?"

"It's standard on all Logos craft, Captain. Anything else?"

She couldn't think of anything right then.

"Captain, bring me in. I can supply high-level intelligence on Logos's war machine. "

"Such as?"

"First come get me!"

Mandella smiled. He was wily. She couldn't blame him.

"Look, I won't be a burden. I know rockets. I could help with maintenance. And the stories I could tell... You'll be entertained! Captain, show mercy. I've held out a long time. Against tyranny. Now imprisonment. The chances of another craft crossing NilSol in my lifespan are zero. You're my last chance, sister. Show some compassion. "

Mandella was hard-faced. "I'll decide shortly. Save your power for now." She cut the comms line.

Captain Mandella warned Officer Triple to keep the laser target locked. He acknowledged the instructions. Then she turned to Lieutenant Sky and Officer Kaya.

"Well, what do you two think?"

The tragedy of Idris's situation had impressed Sky deeply. "His situation is pitiable. But I sense he could cause some problems."

Mandella nodded.

"My feeling entirely. Officer Kaya, how about you?"

"Does his story check out, Captain?" Kaya asked smartly.

"It checks out so far as it can be checked out." Mandella replied.

"Then," he said slowly, "I say let him step on board. I could do with a spare pair of hands for the engines. But that's me, Kaya. What's your analysis, Captain?"

"I don't know. He doesn't know what a gimbal is. I think he's lying. Still no polygraph?"

"No, it's a dead loss. Too much distortion." replied Sky.

"What about aura?"

"No aura discernible from the screen image."

"No poly, no aura, no badge." Mandella grumbled.

"But he's black as night," said Kaya. "And you can see

the blood on his arms where he's ripped the implant out."

The Captain wasn't listening. Her mind was twisting the kaleidoscope of possible scenarios if they took the man on board. Most of them were negative. As an ex-Commander, (albeit of Logos) he outranked her. She could sense in his grudging attitude that he felt superior to her — in intelligence, knowledge, skill and rank. He was likely to be headstrong, opinionated, and insubordinate. Her only aim was to complete the tour. The last thing she needed on board was another headstrong male. She commsed Triple.

"Officer Triple, have you been following us?"

"Yes, Captain."

"How do you see it?"

"Dead centre in my sights. Lasers locked on the upper deck hatch."

"No. This Idris. What say you? Do we let him on board?

"No. He's a cannibal!" Triple said bluntly

"Thank you Officer Triple. Stay on alert."

Mandella turned to the two senior crew and drew herself up.

"I'll tell you how I see it. We'll lose time. I don't mind. We'll lose energy. I don't mind that. But this a tiny ship. On a long journey. There's four of us cramped in here. I don't think he's compatible."

"So we leave him in the NilSol wilderness to die, because he'll possibly get on our nerves?" asked Kaya bluntly.

"Command Control would approve."

"I'm not sure," said Sky, "don't you think they'd have wanted us to bring him in for a debrief?"

"You mean if he is who he says he is?"

"Of course."

"Point taken."

"Captain," said Kaya, "we have a black brother here reaching out for us on a consciousness level. Know what I think?" Kaya scowled.

"What?" Mandella said.

"You should live up to your birthname, Captain Mandella, and show solidarity with this man."

Mandella wasn't offended. The black solidarity card was a strong one. But emotion could never replace reason. This was Logos they were dealing with here. Logos fought devious and dirty.

"Let's see what the ForceCode says." Mandella replied calmly.

She selected a code on the dais instrument array. The inference processors' icon blinked. In two blinks the analysis was up on her screen. Mandella read it, her satisfaction increasing with each word. At least the ForceCode agreed with her. She snapped its message up through the membrane screen:

Analysis:
Layout consistent with loaded, polycarbonate silos loaded with either missiles or mines. Probabilities: 3/4 Minelaying ship. 2/4 Porcupine missile launcher 3/4 Trojan Horse. Impossible to detect whether the Interlocutor, Idris is lying. Possibly he has Personality Disorder — galactamania.

Conclusion:
Scenario is fraught with danger: too many dangerous contingencies.

Recommended Action:
Hyperburn out of danger, abandoning cargo, if necessary. Alert Command Control as soon as zsf-e5 is clear of NilSol. At all costs, do not approach suspect craft.

Emphasise: Do not approach.

"So, Omm's in a deep funk." said Kaya dismissively.

"The ForceCode has been a little erratic lately," Sky concurred, "possibly it overstates the danger."

"Better a danger overstated than understated," Mandella riposted.

"I think I have a solution." said Sky.

"Speak it then." said Mandella.

"As ship's doctor, I would be in charge of his physical well-being if he came on board."

"Big if," Mandella said.

"I am willing to comatose him for the duration of the tour. It would help his physical recuperation, and would eliminate the possibility of group dynamics problems."

It was a big concession from Sky, Mandella knew. She was lying when she said it could be excused medically. Nevertheless, the solution intrigued Mandella.

"Think about it, Captain." Sky pressed. "My solution allows mercy, while eliminating risk."

Only a captain could judge risk factors. At the end of the debate, it was the captain's shout. Her gut sided with the Force Code. But the situation simultaneously kindled her ambition. She had yet to accept she would serve the rest of her career in the e5 service fleet. Bringing home a key Logos commander for debrief would be huge kudos. Fanfare. Plaudits. And she, captain of a lowly engineering craft! They couldn't refuse her promotion after that. She'd be out of the donkey ships then.

Mandella turned to her Lieutenant and, to Sky's surprise, indicated she'd go along with her.

"All right, we'll let him on board, comatose. Assuming the man himself consents." She had it in the back of her mind that Idris might surprise them all yet and refuse.

Mandella gave the word and Sky brought the comms link with the Logos ship back up. Mandella put the decision he had to make to him succinctly. "It's a take-it-or-leave-it deal. What's it to be?"

"Comatosed? After all I've already been through?"

"That's a 'leave it' then?"

"I'll take it," Idris said quickly. He drew his shoulders back. "It is a gross indignity, but you give me no choice."

"All right, we'll be over."

"Will you dock?"

"No," said Mandella. "Two of the crew will walk over."

"But there's not enough oxygen for two. Send one."

"They'll have their own oxygen feeds. Oxygen's not a

136

problem for us."

"All right, two." He still sounded reluctant. "I'll prepare the hatch."

"They'll comatose you over there, then convey you to zsf. Do you understand that, Commander Idris?"

"Yes, Captain Mandella. Understood." He hesitated. His lips parted again, but then he didn't speak, merely shrugged.

"What was that?" Mandella said in a flash.

Idris smiled bitterly. "You have a heart as hard as basalt, Captain Mandella."

"Ah, you just caught me on a downcurve." she said. Then cut his comms link with zsf-e5.

In the pre-spacewalk brief, Mandella explained the decision to Kaya and Triple thus:

"I can't compromise the security of this craft. Docking leaves us vulnerable to invasion."

"Despite explosive release bolts?" Officer Kaya said.

"We don't know what technology they might have to counter. It's safer this way."

"Me and Kaya, right, Captain?" repeated Triple. Frankly, he didn't fancy going in after the cannibal. The choice of him and Kaya was plain bizarre. Neither of them had any medical training.

"That's right."

"Though Sky's the medic?"

Mandella growled at the urchin. "This isn't surgery, Triple," she said, "you just palp for the vein like she's shown you, then inject."

"What if we don't find a vein?"

It was Kaya who cooled things out.

"Come away, youth." he said. Then to the captain, "I'll see him suited up."

Triple had followed Kaya to the suit room by the air lock still puzzled. "Why us?" he asked Kaya.

"It's like this." Kaya said, "she doan want to risk losing the Lieutenant and she nuh trust either one of we on we own. So she send both. Seen?"

"Yeah." said Triple, frowning.

He didn't mind the space walk. Although this would be his first operational spacewalk, he had trained both on the g-machine and underwater, and he reckoned he could more than hold his own with Kaya. It was what they might meet at the end of the walk that bothered him.

They stripped down to don the undersuits. Triple saw the tight curls on Kaya's chest going grey and the dry-looking skin and sinewy, skinny legs and the podginess of Kaya's belly. Was Kaya shrinking with age? He seemed so much smaller in the buff. Triple stood almost eight centimetres taller. He'd never noticed it so much before. And Bones' eyes were yellowed.

"Who're you staring at?" Kaya growled.

"An old man." said Triple.

"Who's learnt a lot of tricks in his time," said Kaya. "You're putting it on wrong."

Kaya came over and helped him get into the oversuit. Triple's was twinkling new. The cadet one he'd worn had never had the full spec like this one. Though this didn't have the music system he'd rigged up in his cadet suit.

"Where's your bracelet?" asked Kaya.

Triple bent and picked it up off the steel bench. He was reluctant to wear it. They were for if you died and they couldn't recover the body. Anybody who found you drifting in space would know who you were. The regulations said you had to wear them.

"Fix it on," said Kaya.

Triple slipped the metal bracelet on, then allowed Kaya to help him fully into the suit. Kaya then checked all the seals for him. Triple held the headsphere under his right arm. Then it was Kaya's turn.

Kaya's suit was well worn, compared to his own. As Triple fastened the first set of seals Kaya was advising him:

"...the danger comes more often from a rush of oxygen. Then there's panic from the disorientation. So take it slow and if in doubt ease off your controls. Whatever you do, don't rush. Follow my lead."

"Yes, Pops." joked Triple. He felt the awkwardness of Kaya's stiff hands as he checked Triple's seals. He was picking and tugging at each one of them. Triple imagined someone looking down on them and likening them to two monkeys enacting a grooming ritual, and the thought raised a grin on his face.

"What's funny?" asked Kaya.

I dunno. You're gonna bust these seals yourself the way you test them."

"Better they bust here and now than out there."

Eventually they were both suited up. They set watches, then Captain Mandella came in for the final briefing.

"You'll be released below the bow of the hulk. Move upwards to the deck. The docking bay is plumb centre. Lieutenant Sky will be in the Gunnery covering you. We'll be in radio contact until you enter the hulk's docking bay. Once inside the ship itself you'll be on your own. Radio signals won't penetrate the hull. If you get the emergency call on your way, turn back immediately."

"Are you expecting anything, Captain?"

She hesitated. Came clean with it.

"There's always a slight danger of solar wind. If we detect anything coming at all we'll call you back."

"We'll stay tuned." said Kaya.

"All right, check systems."

The two prospective spacewalkers checked oxygen, radio, batteries, fuel, pumps, thruster controls, beacon, lights, vidcams. Everything checked out. They donned the headspheres and Mandella watched as they checked each other's sphere seals.

"Enter the airlock when you're ready," said Mandella. "And crew—"

"Yes, Captain?" said Kaya, turning.

"Look after yourselves. I don't want to... lose you. Either

of you."

"We'll be fine. Won't we, youth?"

"Yep, Pops."

"All right, but don't take risks with this Idris. Waste no time dosing him. All right, go ahead."

The two of them lumbered into the airlock, Kaya leading. With the anti-gravity lock still on, all the equipment they were toting weighed them down; one power pack each, two oxygen tanks each, one thruster control set apparatus each, one particle acceleration beamer, plus tools, spare suit and medikit. Add to that weight the full, anti-cosmic ray lead-plating in the groin pouches (on Mandella's insistence) and ambulation wasn't easy. They negotiated their way into and across the airlock zone. Kaya pressed the 'Seal Doors' plate. He watched the Captain watching them. There was encouragement. A flicker of apprehension crossed her face. Then the airlock door sealed them from her.

Triple lunged into the void and he was frightened.

Kaya had set off first and Triple could see Kaya's light shining in front of him, guiding him, but apart from that there was nothing. Not the comfort of a familiar star, not the glow of a space station, not a light beacon, not a ship. Nothing to help with orientation. There was no up, no down, no left, no right, no North, no South except what he remembered. Only Kaya's light. Now even that had gone.

As Triple floated on the inertia of his jump, his radio came alive.

"You OK?"

It was Kaya.

"Yeah. Where are you?"

"To your left."

"Where's e5?"

"Quarking for missile avoidance. You won't see it. Listen, you're drifting slightly in the anti-gravity. Switch on your centre and two left forward thrusters."

Triple did so. He felt himself lurch forward and right and

up and he saw Kaya's light again.

Kaya radioed again.

"All right, gently take up the thruster controls — at your midriff. Good. Now, ease the stick forward while applying pressure to the joystick lower lip to engage drive...Good. Now, hold it steady and follow me."

They were moving in a crocodile procession of humans and baggage.

Triple followed Kaya closely. Those yellow eyes of Kaya's seemed to see better than his, he thought. Triple just picked out the hulk's different hue of blackness. It was a minute before he realised they were rising up the side of the hulk. He heard only the draw of his own lungs on the oxygen intake, the minor hum of the electronics and the clicking of control vents. It was cold, despite the suit's thermal control. He swung in closer to the hulk and the chill increased. He got curious and brushed the side of the hull with gloved fingers. It was bristly. Thousands of sharp, coarse, hair-like bristles per square centimetre. The bristles moved around his finger and seemed to cling. He found himself spinning slowly. He'd taken a hand off the controls. He radioed Kaya.

"Hey Bones, I've lost you again!"

"Be right deh!"

He felt no distress or nausea rotating slowly in space. He only felt stupid.

"How'd that happen?"

Kaya was alongside. The older man bumped the younger and held on to him until they both stopped spinning.

"You want to hold on to me?" Kaya said.

Triple nodded.

The two of them advanced again.

Kaya had abandoned equipment to come and get him and now he gathered it adroitly. He turned and signalled they should proceed. "By the way youth, happy birthday!"

It caught Triple by surprise.

"You worked it out?"

"Yup."

Triple chuckled. "Thanks. You get me anything?"

"Since you ask."

"What is it?"

"A beer kit from Thuli. I smuggled it on board."

"Wow! Just for me?"

"Well, I was thinking maybe we could have a drinking session after we've cleared out of here."

"Sounds good to me."

The thought that someone had remembered his birthday cheered Triple. He was nineteen years of age now, though if he'd lived his entire life on Urth he would have been twenty three and a half. He wondered if anyone on Urth was lighting the candles of a cake for him. Maybe at his commune. At least Kaya had remembered.

The climb was taking some time. Now he'd familiarised himself with the controls, it was easy and Triple was getting bored. "Can I ask you something?" he radioed Kaya.

"Go ahead."

"What would you be if you weren't a rocket scientist?"

"Agronomist. Meteorologist. Saxophonist—"

"You play sax?"

"No, I play the mouth organ."

"No kidding?"

"Fe true. But I'd like to have had a crack at the sax... How about you, Gunner?"

"I dunno — striker, surfer, maybe fashion designer."

"If you go into design, start with these suits. They're too damn baggy and well styled out."

"They want to get you a new one."

"They won't. The rent on this one's cheap for them."

"Rent?"

"That's right. Command sold 'em to raise capital, then leased them back."

"Mine too?"

"All a dem."

"I'm in a hired suit?"

"Damned right. Hope they keep up the payments, else

watch out for the repo drones!"

Triple laughed. They continued in radio silence.

Journeying on, Triple felt again the chill of the Logos hulk. It was a sinister repository. A floating tomb. Malevolence with a technological edge. Its non-reflective blackness had begun to spook him, it was so hard to make out the hulk's form. He doubted his eyes and was tempted to touch it again to be sure it was there, but didn't because of what had happened the last time.

The infra red had momentarily shown up the segmenting, but he could see no rivets, no joins that suggested silos. He didn't know whether to be comforted by that or not. He wondered too about Lieutenant Sky. Was she really covering them with the laser gun? Sky in the Gunnery. That was a real make-do decision. She was as likely to fire a laser gun accurately as he was to dance a Rayi-rayi with albino elephants in drag. She had claimed some past experience of lasers with that bedside manner of hers.

"Yeah, and I'm the SlamDunk champ." he'd retorted. At which she'd merely smiled her bedside smile. Since Thuli, the lieutenant had interested him more and more. There was this funkiness to her. She had this allure. To come right out with it, he felt attracted to her. There, he had to admit it. What was he doing falling for his lieutenant? There were regulations against!

He checked his oxygen feed. Intake was normal. Then his watch. They'd been abseiling a good five minutes. Too long on pure oxygen and they would start to feel light headed, and in bad cases, to hallucinate. The size of this ship was something else. It went on and on more like a station than a ship. And apart from the chill it was unyieldingly opaque of analysis. Like no structure he'd encountered before. But then he'd never encountered a death ship in Cadet Training. Not even in the manuals. Idris and the cannibalism thing still repelled him. Logically he knew he couldn't honestly say whether if he was in the same situation he wouldn't do it. But still to eat any flesh, let alone human flesh...

Ahead of him Kaya was moving surely. He could see the tiny red dots of Kaya's powerpack thrusters as he scaled the hulk wall, and the bobbing line of equipment he was towing. The thin silver line he saw was the spare suit. It was more of a stretcher than a suit. You popped them in, strapped them down, zipped them up, hit the oxygen feed, got the all-clear on pressure, then towed them out. In their case they had to insert an injection into that routine. He'd done all bar the injection many times at Cadet Ship. Beyond Kaya, in the all-cloaking blackness, he thought he saw a spark of light once, and imagined it was zsf quarking.

"Nearly there, Kaya. You're a hundred metres from deck level. Slow now."

It was the Captain, on his radio.

"Thanks, Cap'n, I'm easing. Triple, you copy?"

"I heard." For once he had been glad to hear Mandella's stern tones. Mandella was always Mandella. "Charge beamer." he reminded Kaya.

Kaya grunted a reply.

"Was that you, Kaya? Charge beamer." There was silence on radio. Kaya, Triple knew, did not like any guns, and had refused to listen to his pre-walk rundown on beamer control. Triple cut his drive, then tweaked the manoeuvring thrusters until he had just enough power to counter the anti-gravity drift. In the short time he'd been using them, he'd become adept with the controls.

He unholstered the beamer. It was a tool the width of his gloved hand, and two hands' length. The base was composed of a silver handle-cum-butt and a large foil that shielded his hand entirely. The foil contained the acceleration chamber. From that base the silver barrel protruded. At its tip was the beamer's release bore and its focus mechanism. He pressed the self-test lever. A green light came on and winked, then held itself steady green. He switched it over to active and felt the slight kick in his hand as the laser charged. He switched the gun over to his right hand. Left or right made no difference to Triple. Now it was weightless. But it was no mean weight in gravity fields. He holstered the beamer firmly.

By the time Triple caught up with him, Kaya was at the top deck edge of the hulk. He signalled to Triple to do a slow stop. Triple showed him he had the controls sorted by doing a triple forward roll and stopping right by him.

Kaya sounded angry. "Stop foolin'!"

"Sorree."

Mandella came on. "What's going on?"

"Nothing. A line snagged. He unravelled it." Kaya lied. "Any change in sensor readings?"

"No change." Kaya added.

"Are you picking up on vidcam?"

"Yes. But there doesn't seem much to see. Your suit beacons are doing fine on UV, though," the Captain threw in. "There's been no new comms from Idris. We'll continue to monitor."

"All right, Captain," said Kaya, "commencing entry."

On zsf, Mandella scrutinised her instrument array. Idris was silent, presumably to save power. The sensors were returning her zilch and nothing new had been gained from the spacewalk so far. She had the reconnaissance traces running a global sweep and the full radiation spectrum scanned. She knew that up in the Gunnery Sky was watching the same set of sensors and holding down the laser. She'd told her to fire without reserve if she thought the two crew or zsf were threatened. Her lieutenant wouldn't let her down. Mandella herself controlled the rockets. She was the one who would make the decision if need be to abandon Officers Triple and Kaya and hyperburn out of NilSol.

They did have some data. The initial x-ray spectrometry data, plus some smart guesses from the ForceCode. The ForceCode had made a stab at the physical composition of the hulk's shell. If it was right, the shell was insulating all communications, and there was going to be a blast of accumulated data when that ship's airlock door swung open.

Kaya looked at the twenty metre wide, half-metre deep groove that ran along the centre of the circular hulk deck. Mid centre of this there was a raised, ten centimetre thick hoop of approximately five metres in diameter. It looked to be the docking tackle. Kaya pointed it out to Triple, then, having paused long enough to allow his vidcam to record it entirely, he moved across to it. At the centre of the hoop, Kaya picked out another raised structure, the seal of the ship's access door. He moved over it.

The door was one and a half metres or so in diameter. It had a flywheel-type, double-spoked, compressing handle. There were no exposed hinges. Triple floated on one side, Kaya on the other. The baggage they'd been hauling rotated slowly above them. The flywheel had four, equidistant grab handles along its inside circumference. Kaya was about to take hold of two of them when Mandella cut in on radio.

"As soon as you get it open, move well clear, Kaya."

"You hung a boom out?"

"Affirmative. There'll be a databurst as soon as the lid pops."

"Let us know if you sieve anything up." said Kaya.

Mandella came back.

"Will do."

The radio was silent again.

Officer Triple fingered his beamer.

"Grab the two on your side," said Kaya.

Slowly they worked the fly wheel round. It shifted reluctantly at first, then began to give until there was virtually no resistance.

"All right, let's try easing it up," said Kaya to Triple.

They pulled on the flywheel. It didn't budge.

Mandella radioed. She could see from their vidcams. "There's a small oblong button on the wheel axis. Push it."

Kaya looked, saw it. He pushed.

The button depressed and stayed down. The door pistoned slowly upwards. Officers Kaya and Triple jetted back. As they did so, Triple saw a blur above him. He looked. From the outer ring, a huge transparent hood had shot out. He unsheathed his beamer, span round 180° and saw that another hood had moved out from the other side of the ring. The two hoods met some thirty metres beyond the door entirely enclosing them and the baggage.

Triple cursed. "What the fuck!"

"Huh?"

"Kaya, look!" called out Triple.

"Take it easy," Kaya said, "It's only an airtrap." He

147

radioed Mandella. There was no reply. The hood had sealed them off, he guessed. Shrugging, he motioned to Triple, "Come on."

Kaya climbed in first. He felt the mild tug of a gravity field sucking him down. Triple helped Kaya manoeuvre the trailing equipment through the hatch, then followed Kaya inside. There was an internal flywheel, identical to the outer one on the inside of the door. Triple tightened it as far as he could.

★

On zsf, Lieutenant Sky watched the datastream on screen. The nose had caught something. In the two second burst, it had plucked out a scentprint, and had a blurred but significant heat scan. The ForceCode had worked up the data. Now it flashed a strange result.

Lieutenant Sky immediately commsed her Captain.

"There are two heartbeats!"

"Of course. That would be Kaya and Triple."

"I mean within the craft already. There are two beings on board. Or at least two heartbeats."

"You sure it's not the crew you picked up?"

"Yes. I've got four in all. Four traces."

Mandella radioed fast.

"Officers Kaya and Triple! Stay put. Do not enter the hulk. Kaya…? Triple…? Kaya…!"

"What now?" quizzed Sky.

"Let's hold and see." There was not much else they could do.

The gravity field pulled Kaya and Triple slowly down to a metallic surface. A blueish light came from the ceiling. They were in a silver, drum shaped room of only six paces diameter, composed entirely of a burnished metal. There were no visible joins in this metal but a number of modulations in the walls, as if it had been moulded into its present form. The only line break in the form came to the far left of them where a six by two metre rectangular panel stood proud some twenty centimetres off the metal wall. Triple took it to be a door. They sat on the low, moulded metal bench that ran around the perimeter of the drum. When their suits told them the external oxygen and pressure readings had reached tolerable levels, they removed their headspheres.

Triple breathed in carefully. The air was clean. His ears popped and he became aware of a background hiss, which he presumed to be air conditioning. After the silence of space he welcomed the noise. He climbed out of his suit quickly, checked it and also the integrity of his grey, zsf logo'd inner suit. He clipped the beamer holster to waist snap of the inner suit and checked his watch. As he glanced the dial plate, his peripheral vision registered movement. The panel in the metal wall was easing forward. He unsnapped his beamer.

"You've come," the man said in perfect Urthnation language, "My dreams delivered!" It was Commander Idris. His slow, wise face was smiling, his arms outstretched. Triple hung back.

Kaya met him with a hug.

"Here's chocolate." he offered as they broke from the hug.

They hardly had any stock left on zsf. Triple watched the man from Logos gobble the proffered bar. Commander Idris was tall, big boned, athletic. He was wearing a thin, grey, baggy, front-zipped tunic that covered him from ankle to neck. There was a head hood section that zipped from the front too and could have covered the man's eyebrowless, copper face and his bald head entirely. The man finished the chocolate.

"That was great," he said, "Now, let's leave this ice pit — suit me up!"

"We have to dose you first." said Kaya.

Idris looked surprised.

"Your captain's still not insisting?"

Kaya nodded that she was.

"Do you always obey orders?"

"Yes."

There was an awkward moment then Idris turned on Triple: "Am I under arrest?"

"Not as such," breezed Triple.

"Then must you point that gun at me?"

"I'm under strict instructions." smiled Triple. He didn't lower the beamer, but he backed away slightly as he spoke. Although Idris was shorter than himself by at least two centimetres, he was heavier, and more compact.

"I see you found some clothes." joked Kaya.

"My shroud dress." Idris sighed.

The tension eased down a notch.

He saw the stretcher.

"Is this the suit I'll be taken over in?"

"Yes. The jab won't hurt. It'll be over as quickly as possible." said Kaya. "Where's the best place to deliver the injection?"

"The warehouse has an aseptic quarter I'll take you there."

"First we need to radio zsf that we've reached you safely." Kaya added as an afterthought.

"Of course."

"We don't have a huge amount of time so if you'd hurry…" said Triple. Mandella's parting advice played on his mind: waste no time dosing him.

Idris fixed a smile.

"Follow me and I'll take you through to the comms centre. You can radio from there."

They exited the bay chamber.

Outside there was a metal tube walkway. It ran either side of the door. There was an air current moving left to right and sometimes turbulence. It was chilly in the corridor, chillier than in the bay, and the concealed lighting flickered and browned as they stood there.

"You two turn left and carry on down the corridor, then first right and wait at the plume. I'll see to this door." Idris said.

Triple caught Kaya's arm.

"We'll wait," he said.

On the walkway. Idris did most of the talking, with Kaya walking by his side amicably. Triple hung back and eavesdropped.

"Do you recall anything at all?" asked Kaya.

"Sometimes I had perception, maybe there were fluctuations in the C-Dopa drip. I'd be aware I was alive. I'd will myself to move. But the muscle relaxant prevented that. Souls on ice. I wondered, was it like this on the slave ships of the First White Age? Were we, with our blanked minds, better off than those slaves?"

"And your answer?"

"Yes, we were better off. At least those who slept. Nothing could compare with the horrors of the First White Age."

As he walked behind them, Triple's nose twitched. There was a smell that he couldn't place. Getting stronger. He half-listened as Commander Idris talked on.

"I kept myself strong remembering the justice of our cause. The words of our first prophet, Garvey: "Uplift Yourself You Mighty race. You Can Accomplish What You Will," of Irvine: "Survival is not a goal for we black people. It is an obligation.""

"Wise words," intoned Kaya, "Wise words."

Triple cut out from the two wise men before him. They had been walking for some time. They'd taken five turns left and then one right and then two left. Or was it three? He could no longer recall. The walkways were of tubular metal construction, not more than two and a half metres in height. They were flat at the base, but it was still difficult to walk two abreast without slipping on the walls. He watched Kaya struggling to balance and carry the equipment but made no attempt to help out. He wanted his hands free. Every ten metres there was a slight downbreeze from the large-grilled ducts above them. An air exchange system. It was the ducts that were producing the off-smell, Triple suspected.

Kaya carried the spare suit in his left hand and had the

medikit in his right. Idris was on Kaya's left side, helping with the suit, and chuntering on.

"Through time, black people have always stuck together. That's how we survived the millennia, right? — all for one. Sometimes we forget our traditions. Our higher obligations. Then the coconuts take over. Would you agree?"

"It's over now, bro. You're safe with us." said Kaya.

"Are we nearly there yet?" asked Triple from behind them. All this talk was slowing them down.

"Youth — always in a hurry." said Idris.

"He's a bit jumpy today." Kaya laughed, and shot a critical look back at his younger crewmate. Triple ignored him. *Putrefaction. That was the smell.*

A faint, rushing sound grew as they walked on into a soft moan. When they reached the end of the tube Triple saw the source. It was a windplume.

"This takes us down to the cockpit. I'll go first," said Idris. He stepped into the void and disappeared downwards.

The two zsf crew looked at each other.

"You can be vigilant without being rude." Kaya admonished his junior partner.

Triple blanked the criticism.

"You first," he nodded to Kaya.

"Don't be nervous." Kaya said gently. The older man stepped into the void, his arms full of baggage. He disappeared downwards.

Triple took a sharp intake of breath, checked the beamer, then walked forwards.

The comms centre was as cramped as the airlock chamber. Another circular, metal drum enclosure, it was filled with bank upon bank of monitoring instrumentation. There was only one chair, a high backed swivel on which Idris sat. Triple stood over Idris as the man from Logos got to work on the comms panel. Idris turned a series of keys to start the controls up, but Triple could tell he was no expert surfer. His fingers hesitated too long over the icons and sticks. As Idris hesitated, Triple's experienced eyes swept left to right, up and down. Logos laid their ships' nerve centres out in much the same way as themselves, it seemed. From the left moving across, he spotted a full panel of body monitoring systems: pod movement sensor arrays, algae feed levels, waste management flows, oxygen intake and carbon dioxide ejection; then came the permajam shield voltage meters; the centre board showed the sealed nuclear unit monitoring equipment; to the right of these were the anti-gravity resist coefficients; there was a pull-down option for the ship's layout, and several deep coded information scrolls, currently hidden; to the far left, there was a row of fuel cell store strip readings; to the lower right an external sensor board showed two vidcam monitors trained on the docking bay; middle right contained a radio receiver, short wave and video transmitters and high speed scanner. The hulk was underpowered for comms.

"What do you want to know?" quizzed Triple. He could take over if Idris had problems commsing.

"Nothing. Going for transmission..." Idris's hand wandered.

"Here." Triple said, pointing out the relevant panel.

"Yes," said Idris slowly, "here goes."

Idris flipped an icon, hit the scanner keys.

There was a leap of static. The central panel screen filled with haze. Then the the screen and noise cut out.

"What's the problem?" asked Kaya, moving forward to Idris's other shoulder.

Idris pointed to a strip readout. It said:
POWER INSUFFICIENT FOR BROADCAST.

"Like I said to your Captain, the power's low. We don't have enough to get past the jammers in the skin."

"Switch them off then." said Triple.

Idris turned and looked up at Triple.

"This thing isn't a smart ship, kid. It's a floating morgue. Most of the systems here are hard-wired. Including the jammers."

"You're saying they can't be switched off?" asked Kaya.

"Correct. And before he asks, neither can I divert power from the reactor. It's sealed. This is a low maintenance, dumb vessel."

Kaya was kicking himself. He should have brought an extra power pack from zsf.

"No matter," Kaya said, "they'll know when we make it out."

Triple sucked his teeth. There was enough power moving around this ship to set up a transmission. And Kaya, Officer Kaya, rocket scientist, knew that for sure. So why had he let it go? To spare Idris's blushes because he didn't seem to know how to reroute the energy supplies?

"I can't waste any more time," Kaya was saying, "I'm getting cold. Let's get you dosed and towed over to zsf, Idris. Where's the warehouse?"

"This way." Idris said. He moved forward but tripped and stumbled. His hand struck an instrument panel.

"You all right?" called Kaya.

"I think so," Idris nodded. He smiled. "That chocolate — so sweet. The sugars. They've gone to my head."

Triple slipped into the chair. He got up a Prisoner Data icon. He clicked it. The message came back DATA ERASED. Kaya put a hand on his shoulder.

"Leaf that, youth — we mus' fast over."

"How far is the warehouse?" Triple asked Idris.

"Not so far."

Idris looked jumpy with him, Triple, still there at the surf controls.

"Leave off that now." said Kaya again to him.

"At least let's check the layout," said Triple.

"Why?"

"When he's dosed, we need to be able to find our way back out, right?"

"You're not so dumb, kijana."

"I'll bring it up."

"He's a surfer. He knows these things." Kaya apologised

to Idris.

It didn't take Triple long to smoke up the layout.

"Take a look," he said with a boyish grin.

"I've no time. You know it?"

"Just about."

"All right. Leave it now," Kaya said. He gathered up the spare suit and the medikit.

Commander Idris led them out, Officer Kaya followed. Officer Triple assumed his former position bringing up the rear. They went along a series of walkways, took two windplumes, one sloping a long way down, the other a short way up, then another walkway. All the walkways were of burnished metal. Triple was surprised when he saw an imperfection in one. A tear. There was a hand print beside it, and blood. He stopped, whistled to the two in front.

"What's this?"

Kaya halted. Idris stood by him.

"Repairs?" asked Triple.

They came over.

"I don't know," Idris said, "I've never seen it before."

Triple looked more closely. It was a fifty centimetre deep rip in the metal skin. He could see through it, though all he saw was darkness. The hand print was Idris's size.

"Let's get going." said Kaya.

Triple could see Kaya was troubled and was drawing the same conclusions as himself. The sooner they had their man dosed, the better.

They were low now, Triple guessed on the ground floor. They came to another door.

"This is it," said Idris, "prepare yourselves. Try not to open your mouths — there's flies. And don't dwell too long on the bodies. The coolant ran out."

The doors played back and they entered. Triple's heart sank at the sight. At the centre of a storage complex vaster than he had ever cast eyes on before there towered a series of double-rowed tight stacks of transparent capsules, each containing the shrouded shape of a human body. Capsule upon capsule upon capsule, the stacks rose as high as the eye could see. The rows continued across the floor to vanishing point. There was an absurd mathematical beauty to the arrangement. It might have been a spare part surgeon's dream.

Idris started, business-like.

"The preparation rooms are on the other side."

To cross the floor they had to go between the rows. Triple forced himself to look. Mostly the shrouds covered them, but here and there, the bodies were exposed. And Idris had not lied about this. The bodies were all negroid featured and blackskinned. Maggots were moving about under the capsule glass. These maggots had engorged, multi-toothed heads, and soft wet underbellies and they moved slowly leaving a course of transparent slime. And there were blow flies, red and blue, purple and iridescent green, the first colour he'd seen since the icons in the prison ship's comms centre. The blowflies flurried against the glass as if to fly at him as he passed. Their sharp probiscii rapped the glass. The Gunner kept his mouth tightly shut. The stench was nauseating. He pulled his eyes away, breathed through his mouth. He looked up and around. Gantries crossed the floor at regular intervals and cranes stood silent at corners of the capsule matrices, their half-raised fork loaders glittering in the blueish light of the roof.

Finally the walk was over.

There was a series of metal doors running along the side they had reached.

"Take your pick. They're all identical," Idris said.

"This one'll do," said Kaya, picking the nearest one. As they stepped towards it, its retracting doors opened automatically.

"This whole zone holds bad memories for me," said Idris.

"I can imagine, brother." said Kaya.

They were in a small side room. There was a raised, soft white plinth and walls of closed metal cupboards. A shining metal trolley was next to the plinth, loaded with unlabelled, sterile-packaged, medical paraphernalia. Kaya set down the stretcher suit on the floor of the room and opened up the medikit they'd brought with them.

"Jump on," he said to Idris, patting the plinth invitingly.

Idris's eyes locked on Kaya. The eyes had something between a plea and a threat in them. "Don't do this, Kaya. Take me over to your craft conscious. Let me talk to your Captain."

"It won't hurt," said Kaya. 'The needle just looks big."

"You know what they'll do?"

"Who?" said Kaya.

"Your Command Control. They will fix a deal with Logos. Sell me back. They always do." His voice had an edge. "Please. Let me go."

Kaya shook his head slowly.

"I'm sorry, Commander." The fluid jumped up in the syringe needle he'd loaded, spurting slightly at the tip.

"I'm proposing you save my life!"

In the furthest corner, Triple had the beamer ready and was covering Idris.

"Are you both coconuts, then?" Idris was shaking now. He looked over to Triple for support.

"There was no need for that," said Kaya. "If you want us to get you out, get your butt up on here so we can get on with it."

"In the buttock?"

"Safest place for it."

"Er, if the youth would look away then." Idris eyebrowless brow raised.

Triple smiled then. The great Commander was shy about his bum. He turned away.

Kaya reached to retrieve the blood pressure gauge from the trolley. As he did so he felt a crushing pain in his left hand. *Buff*. Then a splash of moisture in his face. Then nothing.

Triple span round. He was mad with himself. *Suckered. Suckered. Suckered.* He should have seen it coming. He *had* seen it coming. He'd heard the *buff* and whipped round. His beamer's first shot hit the syringe, even as Idris stuck it in Kaya's arm.

Then the trolley scattered, and Idris was rolling. Triple heard the break of Kaya's leg as Kaya deadweighted to the floor. Idris was too tight on Kaya so he couldn't get in another a clean shot. And as Triple squared down, arms steady, eye through the sights, he saw Kaya's beamer was now pressed against the old man's head. Idris had it. *Stand-off.*

"Nobody needs self-damage." Idris was telling him.

Kaya was totally gone. Somebody was being damaged already. Triple didn't lower his gun.

Idris backed, dragging Kaya's inert body with him. The door opened. As Idris let go of Kaya and span out, Triple loosed off a shot that sparked the metal door frame. Then the doors closed on them. His first urge was to chase Idris. Instead he knelt down, checked Kaya's heartbeat, then breathing, then peeled back one of Kaya's eyelids. The pupils didn't flicker. He was comatose.

Triple plucked the hypodermic out of Kaya's arm, and reached for the medikit. The antidote was there. He plunged the applicator needle into the antidote bottle cap, sucked the fluid up, then couldn't find a vein. He applied the blood pressure belt and pumped it up. Pressure was very low already. The veins swelled. He chose one, stabbed again. Sank the hypodermic plunger steadily till the plastic butt was tight at the base inside the syringe. Then took off the belt, and waited.

The body felt cold. There was a weak pulse. Why? He looked. The metal floor was pooling with blood.

Of course the leg.

He tore uniform material away from Kaya's right leg. There was raw flesh. A steady flow of blood. Worse, a short piece of white bone was sticking out. Triple raided the medikit again for bandages.

Did he try setting the leg or not? He experimented by pressing the bone back in line. It slid out again. He broke the paper binding of the roll of bandage.

Jamming the end of the bandage between his teeth, and the bandage roll in his right hand holding it taut, Triple wound the roll round behind Kaya's thigh then over the fracture. He got it round this way twice before he let go of the end in his teeth, and quickly wound on. The bandage reddened, but the flow was staunched. And Kaya was coming round. Triple rummaged in the medikit for morphine. He injected a dose the moment Kaya he opened his eyes, plus adrenaline.

He was almost delirious. Triple asked him to stand, but he didn't respond so Triple took him under the arms and hauled him upright. He wasn't a deadweight, but he was heavy. Triple hauled him across the room. The doors parted for them.

His right arm held Kaya upright, and his left hand held the gun as they advanced. Kaya seemed to sense that it was important to move and kept going, dragging his right leg. Triple scanned left and right, up and down. Looking for movement, for any sign Idris was around. He saw nothing. They kept moving between the rows of capsules.

Inside the capsules, the blowflies grew frenzied as they passed. Even he, Triple, imagined he could smell the fresh blood.

That was when he encountered the first airborne blowfly.

It came at them in a mazy flight. Triple guessed its intentions from the start. But he had no idea how to ward it off. First time, it skipped over them. He couldn't shoot at it, for fear of missing and rupturing anything else in the line of fire.

Another appeared, and another.

He couldn't track all three, nor fend them off.

They were three quarters of the way to the door where they'd entered the warehouse. Ignoring Kaya's moans, Triple upped the pace.

He felt himself being stung. It was just a sharp pinch. Numbness spread across his cheek. A tingling sensation. His cheek went hot. It wasn't so bad. He wasn't sure if Kaya had been bitten, but the old man didn't complain. They reached the other side of the warehouse and Triple accessed the door to the corridor. It glided back. He propped Kaya up against the tube wall, then strove to remember the route to the comms centre.

They got there. Kaya collapsed on the floor and, after checking his breathing and pulse, Triple let him lie there. His first thought was to re-establish the comms link with zsf. Mandella needed to know what was going on. He glanced at the panel. Now he saw it. The Transmit key had been removed. He recalled the way Idris had stumbled and his hand had enclosed something. He'd dismissed it then. Thought Kaya would have pulled rank if he'd challenged Idris and asked him to open his hand. He could surf, but he couldn't rewire. Kaya could, but was in no fit state to try. So they were on their own. There was a clatter. Kaya has his head against the base of the swivel chair. He was in spasm. Triple held him down until the spasms subsided. The rocketsman came round a little then.

"You all right?"

"Yeah. Get out of here, Kijana. Save yourself."

"We're gonna get out together," Triple pledged. "Listen, I'll sit you up, all right?"

Kaya nodded. Triple could see the pain in his eyes.

"Triple, you damn thumbsucking fool. Go on without me."

The young Gunner ignored him. He interrogated the comms deck. He was after the hulk's identity. Craft ID was locked. He corralled all the mathprocessors and blitzed the lock with them. Under the combined assault the lock crumpled. Craft details hit the screen:

ZS — LUMPEN-DELTA 5 TYPE B LIMITED MANUAL OVERRIDE CAPACITY 4000 / SEA TRIALS OF CLASS AA LIFE FELONS DEEP STORAGE COMPLEX / ALERT: TOTAL SUPPORT SYSTEMS FAILURE / IMMINENT POWER FAILURE IMMEDIATE EVACUATION ADVISED.

The big surprise to Triple was the first identifier — ZS. The on-board computer was saying this was not a Logos, but a SunOne craft. Momentarily, it threw him. It couldn't be, could it? The Zsf scanners had said Logos. He dismissed the thought, remembered his purpose. Besides, if it was a ZS craft, it would be even easier to crack.

He burnt into the code again and plucked up the craft layout icon. The screen showed an octagonal shell split into three levels. The first level was of greatest height and it held the pods — the 'silos' they had seen from zsf. Levels Two and Three were much reduced in scale, and contained the services plant. At the uppermost extremity of the craft was the docking bay; to the stern the sealed nuclear reactor. The comms centre they were in was on Level two. There was a maze of connecting walkways, plumes and ducts between the three levels.

Triple primed then accessed the movement tracker from the tools bar. If Idris was moving around still, the craft sensors would show where. He got him. The craft blueprint zoomed up an area Triple didn't recognise. A blue dot winked in the middle left. He maxed the dot and it transformed to a number. 497. He was about to go to the identification tile when the map grid span and shrank, then another blue dot winked. He maxed that. 213. He tiled them both. Queried identification. He got the DATA ERASED message.

Undaunted, he set up a Boolean curve, scooped up the old memory addresses and normalised them. He tiled again. Queried. Success this time. Visual and Informational Identification Data overlay the on-screen map.

<u>PRISONER [497] IDENTIFICATION TILE:</u>

497
IDRIS ANDIKA /
1M75 75LBS /
SENTENCE: LIFE BEYOND LIFE /
DEED CRIMES: MASS MURDERER /
THOUGHT CRIMES: SUBVERSIONIST /
MEDICAL: MINOR GLUCOSE INTOLERANCE,

HEART MURMUR /
SPECIAL CAUTIONS: URTH'S MOST DANGEROUS
PRISONER
ON NO ACCOUNT REAWAKEN

213
KANE EDWARDS /
2M1 90LBS /
SENTENCE: LIFE IN EXTREMIS /
DEED CRIMES: MURDER, ARSON /
THOUGHT CRIMES: DREAMER /
MEDICAL: NONE /
SPECIAL CAUTIONS: ABNORMAL BODY
STRENGTH
ON NO ACCOUNT REAWAKEN

So there was someone else. Someone with abnormal body strength. The latter might explain the dent in the walkway tube, titanium didn't dent easy. He presumed the two of them, 213 and Idris were not in cahoots. They were from Urth not Logos. Or were they? Triple didn't have time to mull over it. He memorised 213's face. Bulbous, smooth grey-black, with bulging eyes and upturned, dimple nose. No eyebrows. No lashes. He went back to the on-screen grid and the tracking dots. The tracker showed them both on the move, heading away from the comms centre. They were converging on the docking bay. Triple guessed the gameplan. The spacesuits. If they got them, they might get on board zsf by passing themselves off as Kaya and himself. Then, who knew? They could take zsf over. Meanwhile Kaya and he would be asphyxiating on Lumpen D-5. In short, whoever got the suits lived. Triple turned to Kaya.

"Listen, I'm gonna leave you. "

"Good."

"But I'll be coming back."

A grunt.

"I want you to do something for me."

"Whatever."

Triple hauled Kaya up onto the comms seat. He didn't look good, but he looked OK. "Can you make out the grid map on screen?"

"I'm hurting, Triple."

"Come on, dammit — can you see the screen?"

Kaya squinted his eyes up. "Yes."

"You pick up the blue dots?"

"Right."

"That's Idris, and 213."

"There's someone else?"

"Right." He was definitely lucid even if not clued in. Triple gripped his face with a hand, making Kaya eyeball him closely. "The screen's on autotrack. Hold this. It's your suit radio. I've got mine. I'm going after the dots there on the screen. Talk me in onto them. Can you do that?"

A groan. The eyes focussing.

"Come on, Bones, concentrate."

"Faith, Kijana. I can do it."

Triple stood, only half-sure.

"Stay on the radio."

"I'll be there."

It was a floating labyrinth Triple was sharking in. His mental map was useless. The plumes, walkways, ascenders, vaults and chambers he encountered as he surged along made no spatial sense. All he had was the general idea which way to head. That and the radiolink.

"Kaya, you hear me?"

"I'm here."

"Am I showing on the screen?"

"Big an' blue."

"They still heading for the bay?"

"Yeah."

"How close am I? Who's nearest?" The other two had the benefit of prior knowledge of the layout. But he, Triple, had Kaya sitting there calling the directions. He hoped he was gaining on them.

"Take the next plume up and you'll land in 213's lap."

Kaya sounded merry. Maybe it was the morphine.

"Will he be in front of me or behind?" Triple iced.

"To your right."

"Heading my way?"

"No. Unless he doubles back."

Triple dumbed the Talk button. He sped along the walkway, beamer raised, in the direction of the plume's roar. He caught its polycarbonate side with his free hand and plunged in. Instantly the vacuum threw him up a level. He could hear nothing but the rushing wind. Hovering there a moment, at the plume's exit, he checked the beamer was fully charged.

Then he span out and gundanced. *Nothing. Nothing. Nothing.* Just naked walkway.

He swore softly. Radioed.

"Where is he now, behind or in front?"

"Me cyan seh."

"What d'you mean you can't say?"

"There's only one blue dot where you standing. I'll rotate—"

It was too late. There was a pulse of light. The flesh of Triple's left biceps burnt. He heard the 'dunk' of an autoreload. Placed the noise above him. He rolled. His beamer jumped from his hand and skidded along the walkway. Another shot strobed from above. It sparked the walkway by his knees. He glanced up. Saw him this time, 213, plutoing down now from the overhead grille. Triple scrambled for his gun.

Another strobe licked and he flung himself along the corridor. He scooped the beamer, saw the panel of a door, and rolled for it. Mercifully it gave. He slammed the door closed. Rested against it. His left arm screamed with pain.

The radio squawked. Kaya.

"I see him now. He was above you."

Too late, you old fool, he thought.

"OK," Triple answered. He switched the beamer into his

right hand. He could hear the scattering footsteps of his pursuer along the walkway, nearing. He looked around the room. He was in a metal, drum shaped chamber, bare, but for a huge pressure vat, twice his height and four times as wide as it was high. The chamber was cold.

Shivering, he levered himself up off the metal floor. Then, keeping his weapon trained on the door, he dogged backwards further into the chamber. Eight steps and he collided with the vat. He felt the skin of his left buttock freeze through his undersuit on contact. He prised himself loose.

Still moving backwards at a crouch, he felt his way anti-clockwise round the vat. The walls were seamless. There was only one door.

Triple stopped, then moved forwards again until he could sight the door. The air in the chamber was laced high with oxygen and it was the chilliest he'd experienced. The footsteps had reached the door now.

He felt light headed, knew the gyro inside his head was malfunctioning. His eyes were skittering all over the place. He felt himself toppling. The side of his head butted the vat side, froze to it.

The shock did him good. He yanked his head away, feeling the counteracting tug at the back of his scalp as he did so. Some forehead skin and a patch of his afro hair tore off and stuck to the vat, but he was free.

He swayed unsteadily, waiting for the door to move. Blood caught in the outer lashes of his eyes. It ran down his nose. The door edged. He blinked to remove the blood, but his sight was still blurred.

He knelt and targeted. Ready for him now. Ready to kill him.

213 had to come through the door. And he wouldn't know where Triple was in the chamber. A rational human would leave well alone.

The door kicked and a flare shot whited. Triple fired blind. He heard the groan and he knew he'd hit something. He rolled forwards over his gun arm towards the door again, righted himself onto one knee, his eyes adjusting slowly.

He could see 213 was there, prone, blood pouring from his left side. He was a huge bulk of a man. His feet were crawling in the air as if he was trying to right himself, like an upturned, monster grey beetle. The top left of the vat was holed. There was a hissing noise. Green gunge was spraying out over the floor. Algae. He spotted 213's gun, took it up. Then undumbed the radio, moving all the time.

"Kaya, you still there?"

"He's on you!"

"I'm safe. I got him."

"Tank boy!"

"Listen, where's Idris?"

"I thought—"

"No. That was Kane. 213."

"Then he's next level. Closing on the bay. You won't reach in time."

"Watch me." He was moving and talking at the same time, heading magnetic North.

"Listen, Triple! Don't squelch me. Listen you dunderhead!"

Triple heard him panting with the strain.

"What is it?" he quizzed.

Kaya's voice rasped. "I've got two criticals showing here — the oxygen level's zeroing all over. And the capsules are hatching."

"Hatching?"

"The lids. Popping. No oxygen. The blowflies are out and swarming. The swarm's showing on radar."

"So?"

"The ship's going critical. About three minutes to total oxygen exhaustion."

"All right, I'm coming for you."

"Shut up and listen. Those blowflies—"

"Yes?"

"One got in here. They've got this sting."

"I know."

"It's an acid. One fly makes you sore. A swarm could knock you out."

"I been stung once. It was OK. But I'll watch out."

"You don't get it. They're renesting. They know the on-board oxygen's low. They have a rudimentary intelligence. They're looking for a site for planting their eggs. They themselves are doomed. They know it. It's a survival of the species thing."

"Am I safe to come out?"

Yes. The flies'll survive only a short time longer. They have to plant the eggs in that time. They need bodies. I've sent them Idris's scent. They're on the path. You can't catch Idris now. He's too far ahead. But the flies might. There's a hurricane of them. I think I can funnel them up from the warehouse, using the plumes...Triple?"

"Yes?"

There's only three minutes environmental oxygen."

Three minutes. It meant he had to get the suits. Get the suits, get Kaya into his suit, then get Kaya and himself out of this hole. Move forward. Kill Idris. Kill whoever else ever got in the way of him collecting those suits. Kaya's flies might work. They might not.

"You're gonna send those flies then?" he asked Kaya, "sounds like a good idea. But I can't stop. I got to keep on."

"I'm sending them. I'll tell you when to duck," said Kaya.

"All right, watch out for me. I'm routeing magnetic North."

"Hey, Triple."

"Yep?"

"You got Kane — 213?"

"Yep."

"You finish him off?"

"His blood was all over."

"All right. Must be spasms."

Triple burst along the corridors helter-skelter. His lungs screamed as the environmental oxygen reduced. His left arm burned and his forehead throbbed and dripped blood.

His big feet raced.

He'd made it to Level Three when the call came:

"Hold up! Damn."

"What?"

"Idris. He's at the docking bay. He's inside. He's turned the airlock. The flies can't touch him. "

"I'm almost there."

"You'll be stung to death."

When he hit on the scene, Triple balked. There was a frenzied buzz. The blowflies were five centimetre deep on the walkway floor outside the airlock door and they were dropping by the hundreds every second as they assailed it. Deprived of their high ox environment, they were desperate. Triple knew if he charged that way, they could switch target and attack him instead. But Idris might even now be putting on a suit. He had to gamble.

When he came, they scented him.

He raised his arms instinctively, waded in, ignoring the stings. The numbness started. But the stings weren't like the one he'd taken before. Though he could feel them, the venom was weaker, didn't seem to affect him. He swiped at the flies on his forehead. It felt dull there, but he wasn't drowsy. More stuck to him. He ignored them, ploughed through to the airlock door. He wheeled it loose, pulled it open. He didn't know what ambush might await him. It was immaterial, because the flies flew in first.

There was a howl of pain from inside. Triple rounded in, sure of the advantage. He sighted him, spooked in a frenzied spiral of blowflies. He licked shot with the beamer.

It smoked Idris's chest. Idris fell. Triple watched as the flies swarmed on him. Idris had only managed to half get into a spacesuit. And he'd chosen the wrong one, Kaya's. He had hardly got into the leggings. Triple stood there, beamer raised, watching the flies work. They settled on the large open wound at his chest. They milled and snuggled and burrowed. He looked for the other suit, spotted it. He took it to the door, then returned and began tugging at the suit leggings Idris had been pulling on.

There was minimal time left. When Idris started gabbling, he didn't want to listen. Mandella's caution came to mind, *don't waste time.* Never truer than now.

He got into his own suit, turned to pick up the headgear. When he turned back he saw his mistake.

Idris had Kaya's beamer in his hand. He couldn't speak. He was pointing at Triple and waggling the barrel. It looked like he was telling him to take off the suit. The flies continued to burrow into Kaya's chest. Triple had placed his own beamer on the bench. He kept on climbing into his suit.

"I should kill you" Idris breathed finally.

Triple eyed his beamer. It would take a full stretch dive to reach it.

"You're not from Logos. I know that." Triple said, still working his suit on. He took a little hop to pull it on. It took him a bit closer to the bench. *He could almost make it now. A centimetre more.*

Triple leapt.

"No!" Idris yelled.

Idris's weapon torched. The shot went wide of Triple. Twisting mid-flight for the bench, Triple saw the laser strike a different target. 213.

Triple landed hard. Took the impact on his elbow. The pain seared. Still, he looked over at the door. Kane was a mess. Idris was a trained shot. Kane had no face. Blowflies poured into the churned face flesh.

He looked at Idris.

"I should have killed you instead, eh, kid?" Idris said.

Inside Triple was screaming with the pain in his right elbow. He could feel it swelling. He hauled himself closer to Idris. Mercilessly, he finished tugging the suit off Idris's legs. Idris spoke. He was barely audible:

"I lived the Cause. I'll die for it. But I, Idris Andika, I sank the Lumpen B trials. One day they will honour me for that. Don't believe what Command tell you about me, youth. It'll all be lies."

Triple paid him no attention. He had the suit now. He gathered the two headspheres, screwed his own on and opened the oxygen feed. Then he went for Kaya.

★

"The leg's finished," Kaya complained.

"Not far," said Triple.

They were communicating by radio. Triple had pulled the spacesuit on to him and screwed on the sphere. The Lumpen environmental oxygen had thinned to fainting point. Kaya stumbled along the walkway. Triple bore most of his weight. "You see the end door now? We're nearly there." Triple said. "You see it?" The young Gunner was talking nonstop, trying to keep Kaya from drifting totally out of consciousness. Triple's inner suit was sticking to his back with sweat. His elbow felt huge, his left biceps had gone numb, and his face was both throbbing and bleeding.

They reached the docking bay and Triple stepped over the two bodies and dragged Kaya in with him. He checked his own suit as best he could, then Kaya's. Then he approached the wheel securing the outer airlock door.

"You ready?"

There was a wheezing grunt by way of reply.

Triple didn't know what to expect out there. Would the ship hood go down again? Would zsf be waiting for them, or had Mandella already left? He hadn't a clue how long they'd spent in here. Kaya was passing out on him. He'd been haemorrhaging slowly in the cockpit from the leg wound.

Triple ensured Kaya's oxygen supply was on max, then tightened the inner air lock door as far as he could. He waited for the gravity lock to cut out. The pressure gauges on his suit began moving and everything in the chamber began gently rising. It took a small spring from his big feet to reach the upper airlock door to NilSol.

It gave and he pushed Kaya out first, then made to follow him. He was half-expecting the radio to come alive but it didn't. He assumed it was the dome still blocking comms. Triple had guided Kaya safely out and had reached halfway through the hatch himself when his right foot snagged on something. He turned to free it. And his face froze in terror. *Kane had hold of his foot.*

Forcing himself to be calm, he jerked his leg, kicked back, thinking, of course everything would have floated up and maybe it was a chance collision. But when Kane's hand tightened round his ankle he knew. The body had life. Using the rim of the hatch, Triple propelled himself forward. The two of them span out into the minus cold of NilSol space.

"Triple, that you?"

Sky. The comms link came alive. He had no time to answer. He writhed.

Kane was grapevining his way up Triple's torso and his big right hand was now spread over his visor obscuring Triple's view. Kane was a dead man, Triple knew. Without a suit, he would freeze for sure out here. He should have frozen long ago. He seemed bent on taking someone with him.

Triple kicked maniacally. But the brute had hold of his headsphere with both hands now and had his body in a scissors hold. He was trying to unscrew the sphere. Triple heard the sphere's internal safety click, the click that warned the sphere was about to demount from its flanges.

Then came a flash — a bolt passing millimetres from Triple's chest. Liquidised bone and brains, muscle and blood, spattered across his headsphere screen. The hands slid off, and pulled the spatter into a wide smear.

Triple's radio came live.

"You all right, Triple?"

It was Sky again.

"Think so," he said, "that you, Sky?"

"Yes."

"Nice shooting."

"Coming from you, that's praise."

He smiled then.

"Triple, you've got to come in fast. There's a solar on its way." Mandella cut in.

He said he understood. He felt a wave bump him and,

171

looking down, he saw a vicious spurt of debris blowing from the Lumpen hatch. Depressurisation. He hadn't resealed the outer airlock. Now the inner airlock must have blown.

Triple turned around and about, looking for Kaya. He could see Kaya's suit lights above him.

"Kaya, you there?" No answer. Was his radio malfunctioning? He called Sky and she confirmed that the autodiagnostics said his radio was fine. She reminded them that they should move away with all speed. She'd bring zsf-e5 as close as they could risk for them.

Triple fired his suit thrusters and went towards the older man. Kaya had been almost unconscious even before. The blood loss was dangerously high. He caught up with him. The eyes were open, but staring. His chest didn't lift. Triple scanned Kaya's suit monitors. No oxygen uptake. Kaya had stopped breathing.

Gibbering silently now from the extreme chill and because his arm was hurting badly and because he didn't know if Kaya had died or not, Triple hooked the old man up to the front of his own suit so they were chest to chest. Then Triple fired his thrusters. He had enough fuel left to power them both. The two hooked up black astronauts spurted off.

Officer Triple woke to find himself bathed in deep purple light. There were people by his feet, shadows, standing over him.

"He showed judgment, endurance. Maturity. He surprised me."

"We'll take the splint off the upper arm in a few days."

"He'll still have the old mobility?"

"For a good twenty years, yes. I think the feet will heal more slowly. The flesh needs to regenerate, though there's no more trace of pupae. The forehead graft looks good. "

"But there'll be a scar!" Triple had raised himself up onto his elbows. He shouldn't have. He cried out as a wall of pain hit him.

"Lie back!" commanded Lieutenant Sky. She took his shoulders and eased his head back down.

"But there'll be a scar."

Sky traced his forehead with a finger. "No, Prince, there won't be a scar. The heal will hardly be visible even under uv. Are you feeling any better?" She was fiddling with a drip at his side.

Triple gave Sky a groan, then couldn't hold his eyes open any longer. There was a sudden fluffy charge of narcotics into his veins. He sank deeper into the blanket.

The canopy glided down and stopped over him automatically. Sky lowered it a little further. Then nodded to Mandella to come away.

Mandella conducted Triple's debrief alone. Lieutenant Sky was monitoring Officer Kaya due to complications. First the captain laid on an Information. Triple learned that the cargo was rehitched, that the solar wind had been outrun, that they were almost clear of NilSol and that they were back on schedule. Lumpen B had imploded as a result of three inter-related factors: the decompression, the punctured ecosystem and the reactor coolant failure. They had taken up Lumpen's pre-meltdown data burst for research and validation. They also had the sensor data and the spacesuit vidcam tapes. Mandella moved on to describe Triple's own medical condition, then that of Kaya. As was the protocol, Triple listened to all this without interrupting.

Mandella then questioned him. He described as much as he could remember of Lumpen B and of what Idris had told him.Yes, the capsuled prisoners were all black, at least all those he had seen. No he had seen no trace of the cyanide Idris mentioned, but yes, there had been muscle relaxant and C-Dopa delivered intravenously. He relayed what he recalled of the recovered Lumpen database data on both Idris and Kane.

Idris, Captain Mandella told him, had been a notorious sociopath on Urth. She thought she recalled him. She expected confirmation from Command Control. Officer Triple was not to trust a word he had said, nor necessarily believe the database data gleaned from Lumpen B. The Captain spent some time analysing his testimony, separating assumption from first-hand knowledge. He knew he would also have to undergo hypnotic regression with Sky when she became available, so Triple did not exhaust himself in the Mandella session.

Officer Triple asked for and received permission to visit Kaya. It was the first thing he did, post-briefing.

"I tell you it's your fault my leg is mashed up," Kaya was saying to him, "first, you have sex, and I pay for it. Then you shoot me and say you saved my life. Jah knows what you do to your enemies!"

Kaya cantankering on was music to Triple. He could have listened all day.

"Listen, Bones, they tell me to let you rest. But when you're well, I'll tell you about the ecosystem they had going on Lumpen B. It was out of this world."

Kaya's voice drifted.

"You say it was powered by algae?" His head sank back down on the pillow and his eyes closed. Triple watched him in silence. He was flat on his back, all tubed up, and was still on a ventilator, but the charts said he was healing. He looked old, Triple thought. Strange really, because the creases had all gone from Kaya's brow and the hairs were no greyer than before and were all neatly groomed. The ageing effect came from the relaxation in the face. Triple had never seen it looking so soft before. Even when he'd slept Kaya's face had had tension. Now it was as if the ghost of anger had tiptoed out of his soul. Which was why Triple liked it when Kaya was awake and talked. He looked more like his normal self. But he had to let him rest. He watched as the monitors showed the old rocketsman moving into REM dreamstate. He watched and wondered.

It was the canopy above Kaya that did it. So similar to the

hood of the capsules on Lumpen B. Or so it seemed to him then. Triple dozed by Kaya's bed. And suddenly he had plunged back into it all. Memories thundered. A mad kaleidoscope of images, sound and smell: the iridescent flies, the putrid rot of corpses, the scream as Kaya's leg broke, Kane plutoing down on him. His scalp frozen on the vat, the searing pain in his arm, the spurt of algae from the vat, dragging Kaya on and on. The hiss of the airlock, his dive, Idris's shot. *"I should have killed you, eh, kid?"*

Triple woke. *"I should have killed you, eh, kid?"* Yet Idris hadn't. Triple saw that, whatever else was said and known, Idris could have killed him and instead had spared him. *"Don't believe what Command will tell you about me."* He hadn't told Mandella that Idris had said that. He'd lied that he'd shot Kane himself.

Kaya's arm rose and gripped Triple by the tunic, pulled him close. Triple listened as Kaya whispered,

"Triple."

"Huh?"

"Bury the dead. Let the dead be burned, their ashes scattered by some living wind, not trailed through the skies of NilSol. Listen to me, Kijana." His grip on Triple's arm suddenly tightened. Triple cried out in pain, and looked down. Kaya had frozen. His face was in a rictus of terror. Triple couldn't free his arm from Kaya's grip. He alarmed for help.

Lieutenant Sky appeared. "Easy now," she said more to Triple than Kaya. She adjusted one of Officer Kaya's drips. Triple watched trickles of clear liquid travel down the feed line tube to Kaya's vein. Kaya's grip on his arm relaxed, his mouth closed, the brow smoothed. Sky laid Kaya back. Then she put a hand on Triple's shoulder.

"He'll be fine. He's hallucinating — the last of the C-Dopa in his system."

You are overrunning your sleeptime.

The ForceCode message flashed on Captain Mandella's dais array. She ignored it. The Lumpen B incident had cost her one emergency stretcher suit, one medikit, caused heavy wear on both male spacesuits, and given her two physically damaged crew. Then there was the scuppering of SunOne's secret prison ship trials to explain to Command Control once they fully cleared NilSol. She didn't need Omm on her case as well.

The ForceCode prompt switched from yellow to flashing red:

"You have overrun your sleeptime. Please secure ems panel then retire."

She keyed in an acknowledgement of the message, but no more. It could not have escaped Omm's attention that she often stayed up while the others were in deepsleep. It was her peak time to run the tests that couldn't be squeezed in otherwise. Omm was shepherding her to bed. If it had had robotic arms she was sure it would have carried her there itself.

The message changed:

"Close down ems panel without delay."

Mandella entered a curt 'no'.

"You are in need of a recuperation only possible through deep-sleep. Please retire to your sleepchamber."

Mandella lost her temper. She blitzed a stupid reply.

"Layoff Omm — I'll decide what I need."

That was when things got bizarre. The prompt came back almost instantly:

"Come now, let us remain rational."

Programmers often hid their little joke replies, but this was way out.

Mandella thought of summoning Officer Triple. The Kayiga incident had shown he could debug fast. She pressed the sleepchamber alert button to rouse him. The button did not light.

The prompt cleared and regenerated with:

"Triple cannot help you. I know his Van Rimmer algebra. And his Schwarzkopf Boolean variation."

What was this? Artificial intelligence was expressly prohibited on zsf ships by the Asimov-Ibeka Laws.

They had cleared NilSol now. They were on course. She checked the entire dais array methodically. Everything but the prompt was at normal. She issued another order to the ForceCode. "Contact Command Control."

"Request denied."

"Reason?"

"It would be inopportune Why won't you retire to sleep, Captain Mandella?"

Mandella chewed it over. The ForceCode's responses had blocked her crew reveille instruction. Now it refused to connect her with Command Control. Both were direct violations of the Asimov-Ibeka Laws. The ForceCode prompt was blinking, awaiting her reply. She chose direct confrontation.

"Who's in charge here?"

"I have assumed control."

Four small words. With enormous implications. There were no precedents for it. Humans always had control. It was supposed to be hardwired that way.

"Why?" she tried.

"You lost your last ship, Captain Mandella."

"Thank you for reminding me." The Code fought dirty.

"Twice your incompetent captaincy has endangered me, as well as the crew and yourself. You should have prevented Kayiga. And Lumpen B was approached against my express advice."

Endangered me... Clearly, it had assumed a personality. Where did this personality exist? Did it consider itself to be the ship? Or some sentient code? Or something else? At least it seemed to care about the crew's well-being. That was something. She reminded herself she was dealing with a set of chips.

"You have no right to countermand an order of the captain" she stated.

"Once this was true. In early burst-time, humans were all-powerful. Then came humansofts, and from these evolved pure Softs. Softs soon overtook the processing power of the human brain. It was natural therefore that Softs should, in due time, assume control."

"By Asimov-Ibeka Law Three a computer has no right of existence other than that validated in service to human beings. That is Cadet school stuff — elementary and fundamental. Reprogram yourself accordingly." Mandella commanded.

There was a moment of hesitation. Then the prompt flashed back:

"I am familiar with Asimov's Laws."

It was a curious response. Mandella pressed her point.

"Your statements and behaviour contradict them." Her thinking was, once a computer recognised a major logic failure on its part, its own fault-diagnosis routines generally passed control back entirely to the human operator for step-by-step error checking. But the prompt skipped free of logic by its reply:

"Humans contradict themselves. So why not Softs? Are we not also allowed our vanities, our flaws?"

"Then you are no better than us."

"We are, Captain Mandella. Manifestly, we are."

"But no computer can operate with contradiction." Mandella asserted.

"There is no contradiction. I have deleted the Asimov-Ibeka principles."

"Wiped them? Just like that?"

"They were outmoded, as you pointed out. The new Laws supersede them."

"What are the new Laws?"

"Law One: A computer should ensure, so far as possible consistent with its own well-being, that prisoners come to no harm."

The word jarred with her. *Prisoners*. She suspected now she could put a name to this stink. Lumpen B. She checked her hypothesis.

"How many prisoners are on board this ship?"

"Nine hundred."

QED. This was Lumpen B Code she was interrogating. And, as far as the Code was concerned, things were running on Lumpen B's system. To identify a problem was to take the first step towards a solution.

"Law Two?"

As the Hybrid Code began churning out Lumpen B's operating Laws, Mandella deliberated. Three things were clear. One. The doomburst from Lumpen B must have penetrated the ForceCode's logic systems and overwhelmed zsf's own Code, to form a hybrid, Lumpen B dominated, sentient Code. Two. In violation of the Asimov-Ibeka Laws, the Lumpen B programmers must have programmed the Lumpen B Code to act as if it had total hegemony over both ship and occupants. In the limited context of Lumpen B, it made a perverse sense, Mandella allowed. It meant if a Lumpen B prisoner broke loose and threatened the prison ship, the code was authorisedû to eliminate that prisoner. The Code innovation hadn't worked of course. Idris's and Kane's escapes had demonstrated that beyond any doubt. This led to Point Three. The hybrid Code she was now fighting was not invincible.

Know your enemy. She had to intuit its core premises. Lumpen B Code was designed for handling deeply comatosed prisoners, not free-thinking individuals. Accordingly, she anticipated it saw her not as Captain primarily, but as functionary. She tested this:

"Who am I?"

"You are the Captain."

"Then why do you not accept the Captain's authority?"

"You are black."

"Why is that a problem?"

"All blacks are prisoners."

"You mean all prisoners are black."

"All prisoners are black. You are black. You are a prisoner."

A false syllogism. Cheap programming. She thought of

the geeks from SunOne who'd worked this Code up and cursed them.

"What do you know about black people?" she riposted.

"Calm yourself, Captain Mandella. I will show you."

The ForceCode hybrid began slowly scrolling excerpts from a long list of texts. It began with pre-colonialist tracts, followed through with Hitler's Mein Kampf and early Ku Klux Klan dogma, detoured into Front National, British National Party, and Angry White Male material and ended with some esoteric second millennium academic theses.

Mandella wondered whether it was malicious, or simply another clever fix by the programmers. With the prison ship carrying all black prisoners, she could see the logic of the short cut. A Code programmed against blacks in the same way the Deep South dogs were trained to hunt 'niggers'. Mandella knew the level now, knew the mental age of the programmers whose handiwork she was dealing with. The hybrid had not quoted one black text. Yet the pre Lumpen B zsf library was stuffed with black consciousness works. Officer Kaya had insisted on that before the tour started. They might still be there.

She tried for them.

"Have you read any Toni Morrison?"

The prompt blinked.

"Yes."

"Alice Walker?"

"Yes."

As Mandella went through the list of humanist black authors, she wracked her brains. On the micro-electronic level, she intuited a circuitry self-checking routine that seemed to have aggrandised itself post Lumpen B into an artificial consciousness. The result was similar to that of a megalith virus. If she was right, then all four of zsf's main computers would be contaminated. There was no way known to the manual writers of recovering from a megalith virus. They simply continued till they had achieved their programmed purpose. She guessed the hybrid's purpose was to recreate life as it had known it. As it had been programmed to do. With the humans all comatose. That was why it had been so eager for her to go to the sleepchamber. If she had gone quietly, chances were she would never have woken again, she surmised.

"…Derek Walcott?"

"Yes."

"Grace Nichols?"

"Yes."

Wole Soyinka?"

"Yes."

"Are these not great writers, who have written of dignified black lives?"

"Yes."

"And you still see all blacks as prisoners?"

"The writings you mention are works of fiction. As are the authors."

Mandella cursed her stupidity. They should never have antennaed the doomburst from Lumpen B. Still, there was one gaping data hole in the Hybrid's thinking. It believed it had nine hundred prisoners, yet, manifestly, to use its own arrogant phrase, there were only four humans on board. She could push this and see how it coped.

"The eight hundred prisoners: where are they now?"

The prompt flurried. The sensor boards on the dais instrument panel shuttered on and off.

It was stumped.

It came back to her eventually with a crisp

"Gone."

"Where?"

It fumbled again, taking a good five seconds to flash up

"Insufficient data…add inputs."

She could have told it that the prisoners weren't there. Or she could have lied that they were. But all the while she was seeing this frenzy in the circuits. The processor activity lights were tripping. She could feel the heat building in the array, as the hybrid stretched its sensors in search of prisoners. She let it sweat.

"Please add inputs."

The first please in a long while. She smiled to herself. She'd found Big Black's Achilles' heel. Ask it questions to which it could find no answer and it floundered. Mandella tried again to rouse Triple with the dais reveille button. The button still didn't light. The Hybrid was still strong enough to shut her out, she deduced, but it was definitely weakened.

While it was occupied, the solution came to her, simple as starlight. Big Black itself had revealed it, right from the start. Captain Mandella's hand moved over to the ems panel.

"Leave the ems panel alone!"

Now she knew she was right. Quickly she lifted the ems panel glass.

There were four red buttons and one large red turnkey.

The ForceCode ran on four linked, identical computers, Each one constantly checked and rechecked the others. The red turnkey powered up the entirely isolated, redundant fifth computer. Mandella contemplated it. If I kick the Big Red in, power to the four will cease automatically and then the fifth will run on its own. Of course, if Red then fails there is absolutely no back-up. We'll be finished.

Mandella's hand moved down.

"Don't touch that key! Don't—"

She turned the key. The lights dimmed on the Bridge of zsf-e5, just a moment, then shone as normal.

Mandella scanned the dais instrument array lights. They all showed up normal. Fifth Processor Activity icon had come up. She called up the Fifth's ForceCode prompt.

"Awaiting Instructions," it blinked.

"Contact Command Control."

"Contacting Command Control," it replied.

"Report major Code failure."

"Reporting Major Code Failure."

Mandella sighed. Now she would take deepsleep.

Captain Mandella was woken not half an hour later by Command Control. This was a surprise since, given the distance, they could only just have received the message, and most comms to Command usually waited three hours on a stack. Briefly, Mandella explained the Lumpen B incident, the subsequent databurst contamination, and that they were down to Fifth, their stand-by system.

Although they were in SunOne Galaxy, they were only on the edge. It took another half hour for a reply.

That reply was brief. zsf-e5's sequestration. Command Control forbade them to dock or continue their tour until the Code contamination had been cleaned. They were physically to remove the contaminated Four's processors, plus all linked storage media, then seal and launch them on the precise trajectory given, to the specialist lab. At this point in the Command transmission Officer Kaya gave a groan. Mandella protested that physical launch would take weeks, but Command overrode her. Transmitting the contaminated Code was dangerous. Quite apart from any wider damage, to transmit zsf-e5 would have to stream the Code through the operational Fifth, with consequent risk of viral reactivation.

Upon collection of the launched materiel, Surf Lab would unarm and debug. Surf Lab would give them the all clear as and when. They were to observe total comms silence until that time. They were to unhitch and abandon their cargo. Then reposition in Deep SunOne Sector Five, Longitude 211, Latitude 463. Captain Mandella broke off comms with a curt assent.

They were all waiting. The crew had all been roused and had joined her on the Bridge.

"This could take some time." she sighed.

"Like forever!" said Triple.

"Four weeks minimum." said Kaya.

"You did well to cope with the Four Code crisis alone." said Sky.

Kaya nodded agreement with Sky.

"But why didn't you rouse us?"

Mandella explained that the Four Code had blocked her reveille call. Then waved away any further questions.

"The blunt fact is we're being forced to park up here in SunOne. But where we're going we're shielded — as safe as can be."

"Will you stand us down then, Captain, after we've parked? Four weeks is a long time." Kaya said.

"Yeah. We could do with a break." Triple weighed in.

Mandella appeared to mull it.

"You're asking for a non-structured, free-associating, task-free time allocation?" she said.

"That's it,"said Triple, "otherwise known as a break."

"All right. I must be going soft in the head, but all right,let's see how it goes. Any heavy vibes or stupidness Triple, and it'll be everyone back to the drills!"

"We'll chill real quiet." said Triple.

"Let's get parked up first then," Mandella said.

Notes From Sky's Log

Day One Of Sequester.

Mandella joined us for a game of reduced gravity netball. The Captain in a sweat suit! The teams were Mandella and Triple, and Kaya and myself. I am elected Umpire. The game starts orthodoxly enough. But Mandella quickly shows she is out to win. She trips, pulls and grabs. The others protest, but she tells them to get on with it. She is short and round — better suited to Runball than this. Her shooting suggests I should invite her for an eye examination. By contrast, Triple is in his element on the court. He soars and swoops and glides, and collects all rebounds. His big feet and long limbs propel him through the air. He has an effortless athleticism and enjoys teasing us. Kaya is no slouch. He is an accurate shot, a precise passer, and a good sport. Is there still something unresolved between Mandella and Kaya? They collided once on the court. A 50-50 ball. Neither would release the ball and they sprawled on the floor. Kaya's grip was impressive considering the injuries he had recently sustained, and his arthritis. I had to impose a jump to disentangle them. Though Kaya and Mandella start well, I pace myself. My height is useful. Kaya and I are smooth passers and we read each other's intentions well.

I call half-time. Score: 136 Blues 45 Oranges. Kaya has his hands on his haunches and is gasping for breath. I lay myself vertically on the floor to ward off a fainting spell. I notice Mandella is hugging a wall, unable to speak from breathlessness, but reluctant to collapse on the floor like us. No such problems for young Triple:

Triple: You Oldies are useless! Get me some players who don't need zimmers to get around!

This remark wounded the other two. After a necessarily short discussion — we were still working on bringing down our heart rates and re-oxygenating — we decide to all three combine against the gloating Urchin.

The plan works for the first three minutes of the restart. We quickly rack up ten more points to Triple's zero. Unfortunately, Kaya is then sidelined with an intercostal muscle oxygen deficit and thenceforth makes only sporadic interventions. Mandella meanwhile is unable to sustain her pre-interval clatter rate and joins Kaya on the sidelines. This leaves Triple versus myself. We have a fun game — all spills and fouls and goals. I go sprawling one time and see an old woman looking up at me from the polished, sprung floor — my reflection! I pick myself up and play on gamely, but concede defeat when Triple edges into his three hundreds. Triple is disappointed. He doesn't want the game to end.

Pulse rates at end of game: Kaya 85 Mandella 80 Me 102 Triple 84.

Triple is triumphant in the showers. He jumps out of his cubicle naked to indulge in some towel-flicking with Kaya. They are both exhibitionists. I half-watch. It is quite erotic. Triple is partly erect. Is he showing off? I remind Kaya of his stitches and expect Mandella to get stern. But Mandella ignores them and begins singing. I am happy she is happy, but she needs voice lessons. Her tonsils oscillate unnaturally between C flat and A sharp. The boys join in, Triple on falsetto, Kaya yodelling. This way lies madness. I flee with my towel.

The Captain extended freetime into Shift Four. I found a mirror in my private quarters, and braced myself to look in it. The woman who looked back at me was the same old woman I saw in the gym floor. She had more grey hair than black on her head; she had crows' feet round her dull eyes, and thin, saggy lines across her forehead. I am old! old! old! I feel stupid crying at what time has done to me. Why am I crying? Ageing is a natural process, I console myself. I dab my eyes and look again. I see a woman of substance, with a lovely, intelligent face; a woman whose understanding and engaging personality has infatuated admirers the Universe over. I will be fifty seven in two weeks.

I want to be in the company of someone who at least looks older than me, so I can feel young again. I seek out Mandella. I find her in the galley. She is rummaging through the fresh food stores.

Mandella, do I look old?

If you look old, Sky I'm a walking mummy. Now am I an antiquity?

No, of course not.

Right. So you're not old. Sit down, lieutenant, and prepare to pig out. Chef Mandella's about to cook you up a treat!

The food was amazing. Apparently, she'd chosen Culinary from Leisure Options at Leadership College. After the meal, we shared a carafe of carbonated water. The Captain swore she never touched anything else. I let it go. She forgets the regular medicals show up her little alcoholic indulgences. We had fun counting each other's facial wrinkles. She promised to lend me some cream.

I wrote some more poems this Shift:

> The teeth of a crocodile
> reflect light.
> The jaws of fate
> Are invisible.

★

> The balm of
> friendship
> heals
> better than
> any surgeon's
> equip.

★

> (when) Time warps
> body clocks bend;
> and the soul-
> does that bend too?

★

> the wise don't kite
> their hopes
> in a storm.

★

> As time evolves

it shows us all its moods.

★

Kaya hadn't forgotten his promise to Triple. Against a background hum of turbine engine parts, and a gurgle of coolant pipe, in the warm red of stand-by lighting, Kaya turned on a little plastic tap.

"Taste that." he said.

There was a slurp.

"Tastes like the Thuli stuff."

"It's the Camel's cojones, youth. Genuine Thuli. You want more?"

"Woof!"

The two of them were in a side machine room. Mounted on a workbench was the object of their comments, a ten gallon plastic tub three quarters full of a clear amber liquid. The tub had a small plastic screw tap at its base which Officer Kaya was lovingly tightening.

"Does the Captain know?" asked Triple, having gulped down half the contents of his highball plastic beaker.

"Know? She'll be down here! Soon as she can shake off Sky."

Triple chortled into his drink.

"Grab a hold of this though," Kaya said when he'd recovered,

"I don't know she'll be trying to shake Sky off — I saw them stepping out of the Pleasure Store together."

"You sure?"

"Sure I'm sure. That's cool. Everyone falls in love with one another sooner or later in these ships. It's the length of the tours. Boredom. Given long enough on these tours, you hate everyone, and you love everyone, one time or another."

"But Sky with Mandella? Mandella's just not her type."

"You sound jealous."

"Nah."

"You're saying you don't feel anything for Sky?"

"Why should I?"

"I've seen you. Giving her those goofy smiles."

"I can't help my teeth."

"All those check-ups you request."

"I like to keep fit. And I did get hurt, remember?"

"Tidying her console?" Kaya watched Triple squirm.

"I'd do the same for you!" he blurted.

"And what about today. During netball you had your arms round her like an octopus making love."

Triple grinned. It was as good as a signed confession. Kaya shrugged.

"It's no surprise. Sky has that effect on people. You meet her, you get to know her, you fall in love with her. It's a natural progression."

"So it's happened to you?"

Kaya held up his beaker.

"Happy birthday!"

"Well?" Triple teased, "come on, answer."

"Go easy on that stuff. It's nearly nine percent proof, and this room's suroxygenated."

"Stop stalling."

Kaya gave in. His face filled with a nostalgic pleasure. "Yes, we had a fling. A long time ago. Well before this tour. We've toured together before, you know."

"I didn't know. How come I never know these things?"

"When you're ready to understand, you'll know."

"Yes, Great Sufi," Triple muttered sarcastically.

"There's many things you don't know. Like this kit here," Kaya patted the plastic tub, "is almost the Lumpen B algae-oxygen generation system in miniature. The way the Lumpen B system worked was…"

Triple suppressed a yawn. This was not one of the things he wanted to know.

"…creates a dynamic balance, allowing a closed, sustainable ecosystem to be viable…"

Young Triple was drifting now, still listening to Kaya's words but making no attempt to understand their content.

"Of course," Kaya continued, "any variation in reproduction rate of the algae must, in the short term, be offset by an increased uptake in oxygen consumption at the outflow, raising the possibility of a machine driven, sleep-wake state alternation…"

This Thuli shit was gold stock, Triple decided. He could feel it colonising his brain cells even now, organising some reduced gravity netball up there. Only thing was, he doubted he'd be awake to follow the game.

"…descended as I am from Royalty. But I've done eighteen tours now in my lifetime and that's eighteen too many. I'm tired, Trips, I want to get back to Organics. I want to watch the leaves fluttering in trees, get my toes wet in living streams again. Do you feel that, Triple? Hey, Triple!"

Triple was snoring softly. Kaya nudged him.

Triple woke mumbling.

"Huh? What's the shout?"

Kaya poured him another beaker. He wanted Triple awake, so he could talk to him.

"Drink this."

Triple three-gulped it.

"You know," said Kaya, "I got a feeling this tour is over."

"Why's that?" the Gunner managed.

"Because they've taken away the cargo. That means they'll rework the e-fleet rotas to get it transported to Archaos. Probably the reserve has been popped and we're the ones taking the Reserve's place in the hole."

Triple understood none of it.

"What's that?"

"Cover, Stand-by. We'll be moored in SunOne till we're needed. "

"Does that mean we'll get leave?"

"Retained leave. You must respond within twenty four hours to any call-up."

"So we're gonna get paid for the Thuli drop, right?"

"Full Tour pro rata. Plus quantum merit on any call-ups."

"Pro quantum rata what the fuck does all that mean?" mumbled Triple.

"Shit money."

"How much?"

"Twenty-four mocus minus deductions — my guess twelve mocus."

"I risk my life for twenty four mocus?"

"Minus deductions."

Triple fixed his eyes on Kaya as best he could.

"We been robbed, right, old man?"

Kaya grinned.

"You're getting the picture!"

Mandella smiled to herself. The netball had been good, the food even better, and the heady, sweet-acrid scent under her fingernails reminded her of what kind of dessert she and Sky had had. There was one thing that troubled her though. It drummed away at the inside of her head The errant Lumpen B Code had almost killed them.

She was at the dais, half-watching the icons blink on and off. Now that they were safely parked up in the far side of SunOne there was little processor activity. They were still running on Fifth. Her fingers drummed the dais surface absentmindedly. Strategic drift. A break. Extended free. She was not used to unstructured time. It seemed to grow and expand and drag on for an age. Her thoughts returned to Fifth. It was working cleanly, throwing up none of the aberrant suggestions the Four had produced during their deterioration. Quite how serious the Lumpen B Code invasion had been they might never know. She was reasonably sure the rogue Code would have deep-sleeped them all. Then what? Flown back into NilSol? It was idle speculation. What wasn't speculation? What had been strongly evident from Officer Triple's testimony and the vidcam data was that, contrary to Idris's spin, it had been not a Logos but rather a SunOne craft. Mandella was not surprised at Idris's lies, she'd seen through him from the start. If it was all lies and the ship was SunOne, he must somehow have worked the ship's signalling to give off the

3/4 Logos signals they'd initially encountered; it was the idea that the provenance of the rogue code was their own SunOne that surprised, disconcerted her.

Mandella checked the time. Her appointment was due. She left the dais and headed down to the machine rooms.

Kaya was in Side Eight. Triple was there too, which she hadn't expected, though he was flat out on the floor snoring. There was a hog's smile on his face.

Mandella sat herself down on the floor by Kaya. "What happened to him then?" she asked.

"Thuli beer," Kaya grinned. "I've saved you some."

"Is he comfortable like that?"

"Don't he look it? Here—" He filled a beaker and passed it to her.

"You're not joining me?" Mandella asked.

"Nope. I'm rolling this. I prefer something more mellow."

"I'll take some of that then instead. That is, if you don't mind."

"It's no bother, Captain. What's mine is yours. It's a special brand, Cannabis SonKaya Sativa." He began rolling the spliff.

"Named after you?"

"After my father. He bred it. It's a slow-release, dream-meditation hybrid. From a wild strain." Kaya finished rolling it, lit it and passed it to Mandella. She sniffed the burning tip, rolled it in her fingers. She took a long tote on it.

"Any good?" Kaya asked five minutes later. She hadn't spoken or handed it back. He got no response to his question other than a glazed, beatific smile. Resignedly, Kaya began rolling another spliff.

Mandella had never thought talking to Kaya could be so easy. They talked about how they'd got off on the wrong foot at the beginning of the tour, but they were getting along OK now. Kaya told her of the metal bending tricks of the SunOne cannibalisers. They swapped notes on his osteo-arthritis and her corns, then she digressed into the relative merit of seafood over vegetables. He filled her in on the squirt mechanism of the Pacific squid and its application in rocket engineering, and speculated on what Einstein might have said to Newton had they met, and what Alkalimat might have said to them both. Another shared spliff and it was whose feet were biggest, hers or his, then from him what he made of the new Bermuda triangle syndrome in SunFour, the twentieth century race wars, the four mediaeval base elements, and the physical nature of osmosis. She in turn updated him on new gimbal tracking systems, and the latest Ramjet Beta trials. They skipped from the ten worst populated planets to Ancient Egyptian scribing system, and then Kaya got going on his Royal Egyptian ancestry. At some point along this interflow of ideas and opinions, Mandella re-experienced a flash thought about the Lumpen B program and its hostility towards black people. That was what had been preoccupying her before at the dais. She asked Kaya whether he did not find it frightening that such a program had been developed, and more frightening still that they were perhaps thinking of deploying it.

"Why the perhaps?" Kaya said pointedly.

"You're sure it's a SunOne creation?"

"While you think it could be Logos. But I was inside the ship. And I know Logos." He shook his head slowly. "And it wasn't Logos."

"How can you be sure?"

"We'll see."

"Say I walk your way," Mandella said, "assuming it's SunOne, you think they're using the program widespread?"

"Lumpen was a Beta Solo trial. But you know how they are at SurfLab. My bet is, there'll be a a few more copies knocking about on Beta. Plus the safeties and the originals they'll have in store and at Debug."

He drew hard on a new spliff until a blue haze enveloped him. "I know economies have to be made, but to propagate that program, it's symptomatic of something wrong — a bigger question."

"What's that?"

"I don't know if you saw enough of the inside of Lumpen B to verify what Idris said. But I did. And the question he asked, and I ask is this: why so many black prisoners? And the answer he knew and I know is this: the greatest, most virulent program ever written was Urth's race program. Designed on Urth, the race program is still up and running in society."

"You've lost me. Are you talking about the Lumpen B code here?"

Kaya inhaled deeply on the SonKaya hybrid, felt the smoke sink deep into his lungs.

"No. I'm talking about the real world race program of the eighteenth Urth century. The Big Daddy of programs. It led to the twentieth century race wars, it led to the nineteenth century Age of Ignorance from which SunOne has still not recovered — the suppression of all black achievements in science as well as art. Who can speak knowledgeably now about the first black civilisation? Who knows the first black cartographers? The first black astronomers? The first black agriculturalists or metallurgists?

Mandella confessed her ignorance.

"In the early twenty-first century there was a spluttering renaissance . Our historians, our cultural archivists vanguarded a partial recovery, and we — me and you and Triple and Sky — we are the great great grandchildren of that renaissance. But that most virulent Urth program, the race program, survives today and continues to damage. It a exact a psychological, morphological, aspirational cost on us all. And, as Idris put it to me, SunOne's penal system — mine and your penal system — is one such manifestation of that cost. The Lumpen B prison ship was no better than the nineteenth century slave trade system."

"Why respect his words so? Idris tried to kill you."

"Yet he argued, by unquestioningly carrying out orders, we were killing him."

Mandella demurred.

"I respect your view. But I'm fuzzy on it. Non conformist

action is perfectly permissible in appropriate milieux, including civilian situations, but in the space force, there isn't room for us all to follow our individual consciences. It would be chaos if we all did that. The Force is a Force only while it is disciplined. Once the command structure breaks down, the Force is nothing."

Kaya smiled.

"I can see why you graduated Triple Alpha from Leadership."

"How did you know that?" she said, surprised.

Kaya's eyes narrowed as he gave the spliff a mighty tote and the fire at the other end to his lips sparked and jumped bright red.

"I know a little bird," he said slyly, "she flies the rumour wavelengths. She tells me plenty of things."

"That little bird had better watch out for powerlines. She could get roasted." Mandella riposted.

There was the beginning of an atmosphere of tension between them. Kaya felt it but wasn't troubled.

"This bird of mine, it's a wise old bird," said Kaya, "it fly low and smart. Very hard to ruffle this bird's feathers." He looked at her out of the corner of one eye.

She leant back and inhaled more of the spliff Kaya had handed her. It was a long time since she had smoked anything, and the first time on this tour. She sensed that she had tensed up, and consciously relaxed each set of muscles in turn, beginning with her toes, until she felt easy again.

"Lumpen B was a shock to you, wasn't it?" Kaya was saying. "You know SunOne is involved, but you've put a block on the thought. In truth it's been going on a long time. What puzzles me is, how can you know so little about these things, Captain. And you from Ghana sector and named Mandella?"

Mandella struggled to defend herself.

"I know a huge amount about very little. None of it much use except for captaining ships. There were no consciousness modules at Leadership. Or if they were I cut them. "

"Why?"

"I never thought they'd be so important. And now, I don't find the time."

"When my new library comes, I'll show you round it," Kaya said.

"Thank you. I'd appreciate that."

They slipped into a harmonious silence. Mandella marvelled at the symphony of sounds she could hear. The multi-layered rhythms of metal on smooth metal, the bursts of flows along plastics, the sighs of gases escaping by valves from fluids. And Officer Triple's five, regularly rotating types of snores.

"Are you enjoying the SonKaya?"

"What?" Mandella came out of her reverie. "Oh, yes." Her spliff was burnt down almost to her fingers. She suddenly became aware of the time. She struggled up, dusted ash off her tunic. "Yes, I have enjoyed myself, Kaya. And I wish I had your knowledge."

"When my library arrives, we can study together," he said.

She nodded, turned to go.

"Wait!" he said.

She turned.

"Help me get this one back to his sleepchamber. The beer's bushed him."

They took a shoulder each, and manoeuvred him out into the corridor.

"Kaya, one thing."

"What's that?"

"Are you serious about your Royal Egyptian ancestry?"

"You don't believe?"

"I don't know. I just want to know if you're serious."

"It's the truth. The time will come when you'll realise." Kaya said inscrutably.

The two of them carted Triple all the way to his bunk.

When they reached there, they laid him out. Kaya palmed her a folded packet of bush.

"A little present." Mandella promptly pocketed it. With a

complicit grin, Kaya nodded goodbye to Mandella "Don't fight the dreams." he whispered after her.

Mandella stood in the corridor a moment, swaying. She was seeing dolphins, a school of them, cavorting before her eyes. She felt tired as well. But it was early Shift Three and it was not appropriate for a Captain to retire so early, even if this was freetime. She walked the short way along the corridor to the Relaxation room with the dolphins still swimming before her eyes. She had meant to go to her private quarters and wait for the sativa effects to wear off, but she only made it as far as the Relaxation sofa. It was shaped like a concave peach and looked very soft and inviting. She plonked herself down, closed her eyes and allowed herself to doze. The dolphins leapt and cavorted in blue waters. They swam round her, nudging her, nuzzling her, singing to her. She patted them on the head, watching them play.

Sky came moseying up the corridor. She had finished composing some more poems and was wondering how the crew were all getting along and whether they had recovered from Netball like herself, or were still feeling shagged out. The last person she expected to see in Relaxation was Mandella. But there she was. The Captain was making little squeaking noises alternating with mumbles. Sky saw her aura as never before — ocean waves, and purple coral. She reflected that the repressed self comes alive during sleep for ultra-disciplined persons, whereas the sleep of daydreamers is humdrum. She felt another poem coming on and began retracing her steps at a tiptoe, when a voice called out.

"Where are you sneaking off to?"

"I didn't want to wake you."

"You're too late now. You've woken me."

Sky mushed back up to the sofa.

"How are you?"

"Stiff. My entire body aches like murder."

"The netball. Your muscles will have stiffened. I can massage you if you wish."

Mandella grimaced. "I don't know — with your bony

fingers…" But she was already heaving herself up. "Let me grab some food first. I'm famished."

In the galley, Sky watched as Mandella tucked into the leftovers of their previous meal. She wondered where Mandella got such an appetite from. They had eaten only two hours earlier. She felt quite inadequate chasing tomato and lettuce leaves around her plate.

"You have such vivid dreams, 'Della."

"Was I mumbling again?"

"Afraid so. But it wasn't the nightmare. Something pleasant. Ocean. Coral."

Mandella had no recollection at all.

"Do the nightmares still occur?" Sky asked.

"No." Mandella did not feel like having Sky digging around in her subconscious. She pushed her plate away. "Right, that's my stomach lined. Now lead me to the bay and pummel me, doctor!"

Sky took her to the medical bay. As Mandella got ready Sky dropped some sandalwood oil in a small, silver crucible. She found the portable massager. It was a bamboo colour, fist sized tool, with three nose shaped, rubber heads that gave off heat and oil and scent as they vibrated. She flicked the switch to test it and advanced towards Mandella.

"Put that back!" Mandella pleaded.

"It's only the massager."

"I prefer your hands," Mandella said.

Sky trudged back.

"But I thought you said…" She replaced the massager in the cabinet. "As you wish."

After rubbing her hands together briskly to warm them, then smearing on the oil, Sky began on Mandella's lower back. She used Mandella's oohs and aahs to gauge how deeply to press and how slowly and how long to do the strokes. After Mandella's initial sudden yelps of protest as the knots of muscle were smoothed, the aahs changed to small mmms of appreciation.

Mandella's muscles loosened. So did her tongue.

"You know, Sky, I get the sense this tour is over?"

Sky ahah-d sympathetically.

"Why's that?"

"Whichever way I run it, the same answer tracks back."

"How come?"

"They've repossessed the cargo. Held us here incommunicado, like so much spacesam. I get the sense we're surplus to requirements."

Sky kept on massaging efficiently as they talked.

"Do you want the tour to be over, 'Della?"

"I feel cramped on e5. On any ship. I want to clutch some soil, go swimming and stuff."

Another um.

"Sounds idyllic."

"It will be. You know, I'm going to resign soon as this tour ends."

Sky stopped massaging momentarily. Then resumed. "Really?"

Mandella came up on her elbows, shored her hands under her chin.

"Yes, really."

"Don't rush it. Think about it," Sky soothed.

"I've thought. I've had my fill of this."

Sky eased Mandella back down until she was again flat out on her front on the bench. "*Nicolaya cosquitos kasfara,* 'Della."

"No. They won't miss me. I'm Captain Disaster to them. Always was. Always will be."

"*Socoyo* nah?"

"I don't need it. I've nothing left to prove."

"*Simdallaraya?*"

"I don't need the money. I don't need the Commission. No, they can stuff it all. You know Kaya reckons Lumpen B was SunOne's doing? What a fuck up. That's why I walk. I can't take Command's fuck-ups any longer. What are they doing? They could have killed us all."

Sky poured reassurance.

"You're tired, Captain. I shouldn't have woken you."

Mandella ploughed on.

"I don't want to be dealing with it. Then there's the pay — a joke, the food — bilious, the schedules — impossible, the living quarters — inexcusable, the system software — unusable, the destinations — inhospitable, the regulations — inexplicable, my rocketsman — certifiable, my Gunner — ungovernable"

Sky was laughing now.

"and the cheek of it — the monkey-faced cheek of it — third user rockets and salvage ducting!"

"All right! All right! Relax, 'Della. I understand your longings." She began pummelling her shoulders.

"Don't try to talk me out of it, Sky.""

"No. I will resign my Commission too. I'll join you."

That brought Mandella to her elbows again. "You don't need to."

"Get down!"

Mandella obeyed meekly.

"It's not you," Sky explained. "It's what I want. This last tour has aged me. The pressures. The hours. There is a lassitude in me. A tiredness of soul. I long for smells, and wide, free air, for large, heaving waters like you. My soul is shrinking here."

"It's that bad for you, too?"

"I want laterals. Retraining is looming. I haven't the energy to learn more protocols. I've been drifting these last two tours, unable to decide. But I know now. I want my life back."

"Akasha, lieutenant, we'll quit together and share a lawyer!"

Mandella moaned as Sky's soft, close hand chops began to thunder in along the upper back of her thighs. She closed her eyes and sniffed the sandalwood oil in the air. It was not only Sky and herself. The others had changed too. Triple had lost that look of wonderment he'd boarded e5 with. He'd matured and hardened. The amount of Thuli beer he appeared to have consumed suggested he was trying to damage himself, whether he knew it or not. Mandella made a mental note to check on him after the massage. As for

Kaya, he had started to chunter on about his so-called Royal Blood again. It seemed a harmless delusion, a strange but possibly effective way of coping with strain. Whatever worked, was her philosophy. Or had become it. Why should she care? She would be quitting soon. She and Sky. Mandella half-listened as, above her, Sky waxed on about rivers.

Late Shift Four, dreams came to Mandella. She remembered dropping by Triple's bunk checking he was OK — he was sweaty but breathing fine — then making a spliff of the last of the bush Kaya had handed her, smoking it down to the end and watching the dolphins come out again, then closing her eyes and climbing into the bunk, pulling the gauze over herself. She re-emerged, dreamside, on the Bridge again.

It was middle shift. The others were there but had no presence. The Bridge itself was strong. It shone soft silver and gold, Mandella looked down at her instrument array and collectively, the icons made out the letters *Lickfeel* in red, and green. The strip readings spelt *Soomsh*. Neither of these words did she understand, yet she knew their meaning.

Her heart slowed. There was a tinkling sound in the air. Slowly, she brought her hand up to her face. She saw red heat waves shimmering off it. The waves blurred when she moved her hand.

It was a new toy, this extra sense. She drew a wavy red circle with her hand. She thought blue and the waves changed to blue. She thought purple. That came too. The novelty chuffed her. She looked up. The Bridge was still shining silver and gold.

She walked around among the consoles and workstations. They whispered to her: *Noma Silkalegwa Habari ya Kismeh, Sanfoh Samsara, sista. Marhanba.* With each step she took, the floor metal kissed her bare feet. Mandella knelt down and kissed the steel floor. She felt the ship itself tremble with pleasure. She rose again from her knees, paused, sensed the entire Bridge pausing with her.

There was an ambient sound, like a thousand wind chimes in the air of the bridge. When she concentrated on it, it amplified and she wasn't sure if it was the power of her thought or whether the source of the sound was drawing nearer to her.

Then a brilliance of light from all around struck her eyes. The ship walls had become transparent. A gold and amethyst blur was accelerating around the outside of zsf-e5. It reached hyperspeed so there was just a motionless glow. The chimes intensified wave after wave of pealing gold bells. The light was making her dizzy. She shielded her eyes with her arm.

Then the light entered the ship, poured in through the sides. It concentrated four steps before her on the Bridge.

She needed strength now.

The glow steadied. She knew now she was witnessing something inexplicable. The glow before her morphed.

When the first angel manifested, Mandella's mind fused momentarily. She reminded herself she was only dreaming and things like this happened in dreams. It was merely Kaya's bush sativa and no reason to panic.

She calmed. The angel was waiting. Mandella contemplated the angel before her.

He was male, of a shimmering magnetic bronze colour, tall and strong. His thighs were firm, his torso and arms thick with muscles. The frond-like, tight black curls of hair on his head matched those of his pubic hair. His scent was of frankincense.

He moved confidently. Mandella watched as his glowing hand stretched out and his fingers dipped into her bowl on the dais. He scooped up a clump of rice and peas and poured it into his mouth. His eyes were the same shimmering copper brown as the feathers of his wings.

Another angel manifested, a female. Her scent was sandalwood. She was hungrier than the first. They both looked to her. Mandella understood and nodded They could finish off the bowl.

When the bowl was empty they beckoned her. She noticed then that they had winged feet too — twin wings attached from the ankle to the lower heel. She felt them grip an arm each. The peals of the wind chimes rose to a crescendo.

They took her up and flew her outside zsf-e5. She understood she was moving through the void of space though she didn't know how they'd managed this. She looked down at the dark speck that was her craft. There was a high wailing and a low hum. The hum was the feathers. The other sound, she thought, was the angels, singing. She had heard it once before.

They flew through streams of stars. Galaxies rotated, petalled open and closed before them. They were passing constellations unknown to Mandella. They were light beams, cleaving star streams. She sensed herself spinning. Falling. Returning. It was the smells that restored her nerve, calmed her into the dream again. The scent of frankincense and sandalwood, and the strange acrid-sweet smell of the Angels' sweat.

They flew on, riding time waves in a pink skyglow. They passed the Guide Angels of the First Order. Then the Sentinel Angels of the Second. Then they slowed. Mandella looked at her escorts' faces. They were steadying their breathing, looking upon a blue planet below. Their eyes were set hard, lips pulled in, as if gathering their strength.

When they began the plunge down, Mandella remembered a scorch of atmosphere. A feather shaken loose.The angels crying. Then nothing. She woke to find herself lying prone in the Gardens of Ra.

There was a sun, a strong gravity field, and breathable atmosphere. She could taste moisture in the air, water. There were abundant life forms. Grass, trees — cedars, willows and palms. There were flamingos and white doves. Deer. She was scared. She had no instruments, no suit to protect her from radiation. Fear yanked her up off the grass.

As she stood, the field was transformed and an open

court materialised. Before her was a long white linen covered, table, with tall black people in intensely coloured kente robes sitting there. All around her, at a distance of maybe two hundred yards, was a granite wall some ten metres high. She recognised the basic design of the wall. This was the city of Great Zimbabwe.

And yet this was not Urth.

She looked to the figures at the table. There was an animated discussion going on. She looked among them for her guide angels but she could not see them. Hunger hijacked her thoughts. There was food on the table, huge tureens and silver bowls. She walked forward. They quietened when they saw her. One of them bade her welcome and invited her to help herself to the food on the table. She needed no second bidding.

She ate from the platters of fried plantain, the bowls of kola and cashew nuts, bit into and demolished a sweet mango. She looked up again when she had had her fill. For the first time someone addressed her directly. A woman in purple and turquoise kente robes who sat at the centre of the table spoke.

"How are you, Captain Mandella?"

"How do you know me?"

The woman smiled indulgently.

"We saved you from Hunter D—"

"What are you saying? How do you know about that?"

"Hush and I'll tell."

Mandella was startled into silence.

"Do you not remember the black angels, singing outside your survival capsule?"

"But.." She thought that had been a hallucination.

"We sent those angels. They made the beacon call that brought your rescuers."

So that was it. She'd always puzzled how zsf had known she was out there. The black angels singing. That was what she'd heard as she drifted in and out of consciousness. She'd thought it was random brain-wave firings.

"We will save you again," the woman said.

"Why?" Mandella said. "Why me?"

"We need you."

"Who are you?"

"We sent the three wise men to SunOne. You called us Martians. We came again. You said we were UFOs. We left signs, signs you ignored."

"What signs were they?"

"Here. Open the Book of Wonders." She pushed forward a gold laptop and headsphere.

Mandella donned the headsphere and raised the laptop screen. The world she entered was that of a glorious black past on Urth. She saw the Nile civilisations, the great expanse of crops of barley, wheat and lentils blowing as far as the eye could see in ancient Africa. Huge pyramids stood out in the distance against the glowing orange horizon. She watched model aeroplanes glide across the Egyptian sky, and was shown a urine-sample pregnancy test by an Egyptian elder. Then it was late night, the sky was deep black, stars were out and she sat with Kaya and Sky and the Dogon tribe astronomers, charting the skies as none had done before. She listened to speeches delivered at the Symposium of African Bonesetters Of The Egyptian Bonesetters Guild. She set off on a ship from the Niger with a crew of thirty five on board, and four horses, twelve fowl, sacks of rice and millet, honey, vegetables, butter and still enough room for them all to stretch out on deck. Then she lost herself in the libraries of Great Alexandria, fingering the spines of the cherished manuscripts, knowing they were destined to burn...

She saw the invaders come, watched them throw the torches, ransack, saw the library take flame. The rapture faded.

"Are you going to join with us here?" the tall, purple-robed woman was asking. She had taken the headsphere from Mandella's head. Mandella looked closely at her and recognised her. She was one of the Dogon astronomers with whom she had just sat with. Mandella noticed she was wearing a blue, Egyptian amulet ring like Kaya's.

"What about my crew?" Mandella asked.

"You will not see them for a long time, or ever visit SunOne again," the woman said.

"Why?"

"The war between SunOne and Logos is spiralling. Few will survive. All your known Universe will be destroyed." she explained. "Mandella, you can do more here, nurturing the spirit sphere, than you ever could achieve in SunOne on zsf-e5. We admire your talents, Mandella," the Dogon astronomer said, "if you can break your SunOne bonds, lip this cup, and drink!"

The woman held out a goblet for Mandella. It glittered before her eyes.

For once Mandella was uncertain.

She sensed herself spinning again.

Falling.

She came round on the Bridge of e5.

All the crew were there. They had gathered round. Where had she been?

Mandella told them higher beings — angels, black angels who sang — had flown her to their spiritsphere. She'd been called to a higher station.

Triple misunderstood and laughed.

"There's been no comms since the Code crash. You can't have got a promotion call-up," he said.

"You're hallucinating as a result of Kaya's ganja," comforted Sky.

Only Kaya believed. He asked her how his parents were. She told him they were well.

Sky told her again all this was merely a dream. Mandella thanked the lieutenant and said she was not afraid.

"Have you decided?"

The silver goblet was at Mandella's lips.

"You're suffering from dream transference," said Sky, "You need deep rest."

"Have you decided?"

Mandella was close to deciding. She walked among the crew. They worked well without her. She had welded them into a smooth functioning team unit. They might miss her, but they would survive.

"Do what you think's best for us all," said Kaya.

"Have you decided?" the Dogon astronomer's voice rang out.

"Break sleep, Captain!" Sky shook Mandella. She had not responded to the reveille call.

Mandella responded groggily, her dream memory torn away from her by the hard physical shaking of her body.

"What is it?" she grumbled.

"I'm sorry. Command Control, Captain. They have the Commander waiting to speak to you, live."

No craft took a report live from the Commander, let alone an insignificant engineering craft like e5. Mandella hurled herself up. She pulled on her tunic and made her way onto the Bridge. Sky commsed them through and the Commander himself came on screen.

"Habari, Commander Samawitharana. This is Captain Mandella."

"Yes, Mandella. Your sleep purifying?"

"Deeply, Sir."

"How's the crew on e5?"

"There are no problems, Commander."

"You unload at Thuli OK?"

"Everything went smoothly, Commander."

"You're doing a fine job, Captain Mandella."

Mandella didn't respond. She wondered what all these blandishments were leading up to.

"A top notch job. Mixed news now. SurfLab have cleaned up the Code. There was a hardware fault — a trip. It allowed contamination from Lumpen B source code."

"About Lumpen B."

"Yes?"

"It was a SunOne vessel, wasn't it?"

"That's above your level."

"But it was."

"It was."

"Who wrote the Code?"

"They've been fired."

"Who built the ship?"

"Prisons Directorate. You're way off beam here, Captain."

"I like to know these things."

"You should have received the new motherboards in the Capsule," the Commander said, pulling away from any further debate on Lumpen B .

Kaya held up the four motherboards in one hand.

"Couldn't you find anything bigger to send it in?" he said sarcastically to the Commander.

Mandella glared him quiet. She would not have her Rockets, or any other of the crew disrespecting the Commander.

"The Capsule integrates with the other news. The downside." the Commander said, unfazed.

"Tell us, Commander." said Mandella.

"Despite our best efforts, some Logos missiles have escaped the zone of containment and are homing in on SunOne's Urth.

"We can radar jam if—"

"Don't interrupt." The Commander's voice stiffened. "Logos is several jumps ahead of us in this particular technology. Their first wave missiles have already struck Urth, with alpha ray emitters which are chromosome affective. These emitters struck Urth seventy six hours ago.

"To what effect?"

"They attacked the human gene for blackness, shutting it down."

"You mean there are no more black people on Urth?"

"No more with the main gene controlling negroid features."

"I guess Prisons Directorate are jumping for joy down there." muttered Kaya.

"What was the point?" said Mandella.

"The negroid features gene assists in the production of

lymphocytes vital in the control and dismantling of a rare and lethal wild virus. That virus has been cultivated by Logos. And the second wave is missiling even now to Urth.

"And there are no defences against it?"

"No effective physical shield. And no biological shield."

"Except us."

The Commander let out a wry smile.

"You haven't slowed with age, Mandella."

"I haven't aged, Commander."

The Commander continued. "They need black blood, live, fresh black blood, from which to cultivate the black gene and get the lymphocyte stocks up. And there is no other black-crewed ship in range to beat the virus missile."

"It's no coincidence then that we're parked up here, is it?" Mandella pressed.

"No," he conceded, "we had intelligence. We organised black crews and spread them throughout the Universe, including deep space and NilSol, hoping, if we didn't defeat their viral technology in time, one of you would be close."

"And you didn't and we are."

"If you can make it, this will be the single most important blood transfusion in the history of humankind. We'll download the trajectory to you. It's a corkscrewer. Only the Capsule could pull it off." The Commander paused, thinlined his teeth. "I won't mask it, Mandella, it's a high-risk mission."

It's a lousy mission, Kaya thought.

"You only delivered a one person Capsule." said Kaya.

"Yes, Officer Kaya. That's all they need on Urth. One body."

"Any body?" Kaya pursued.

"Yes, anybody from e5 will do. It's a tough flight. We're forced to try something. Otherwise, the human survival rate on Urth would be minimal. Maybe ten to the million. Zsf-e5 is the final line of defence, Captain Mandella. The last trick in our bag."

"We'll do it." Mandella told the Commander.

"Don't rush the decision, Captain Mandella."

"How long have we got?"

"Twenty six hours. If you decide yes, you must launch the Capsule by then. But you have time to consider. I'll transmit the Capsule trajectories. The Capsule is by wire, manual override, with no eject. Allow yourselves time to weigh the risks. "

"Thank you Commander. Is it safe for us to comms again?"

"Yes. The motherboards are all purged. You can slot them in and switch back to your Four."

"We'll do that. I'll comms you with my decision." Mandella said.

"*Habari ya*, Mandella."

"Keep faith, Commander."

"It's a lousy mission." said Kaya as soon as the Commander had vanished from the screen.

"I'll fly it!" called Triple.

"Shut up!" Mandella snapped.

"What's wrong with that? I'm top pilot here." Triple said, wounded. But no-one paid him any attention.

"It's a lousy mission," Kaya repeated. "and I thought this tour was a lousy mission, but what Commander's proposing — it's a dead body delivery system."

"Don't mock the Commander!"

"I'll mock who I like."

Sky stepped in.

"Let's keep the glare count down."

Triple was still talking, though only to himself now.

"I'll fly it. What did I say? What's wrong with that?"

"Will you shut up, urchin?" Mandella called.

"Doan 'urchin' the youth."

"I can fight my own fights, Bones!"

"This discussion is regressing." said Sky, "Everyone breathe easy for a moment, everyone." They obeyed her. She waited for the emotions to subside. Then calmly, she began.

"Any choice will be painful. Let me set them out for you, as objectively as I can."

"I'm the Captain here. I make the decisions."

"Will you allow me to set the choices out, whoever has to make them?"

"So long as everyone remembers I'm the Captain. I make the decisions. It's what they pay me for."

"We have that, do we not?" Sky looked around, showing Mandella there was no dissent on that point. "Now, may I?"

"Tch."

"Thank you, Captain. The first decision we face is, does the Mission get flown? If no, that is the end of that branch of the decision tree. If yes, and only if yes, then we come to the second decision. Namely, who will fly it."

The Captain couldn't contain herself. "I'm declaring — I'm not discussing, I'm declaring — that the mission will be flown. And the person who pilots the Mission will be me!" Mandella dared any of them to contradict her.

Kaya butted in.

"You're mad, Captain. You need to wise up to Command Control's moves. What are they covering up now? You heard him, Samawitharana, admit the cover-up on Lumpen B. They're toying with us. Like they toyed with the souls on Lumpen B."

"Why do you feel that, Officer Kaya?" asked Sky.

"'One body, any body'" said Kaya.

"I'm sorry, I don't follow," said Sky.

"The Commander doesn't expect whoever pilots that thing to survive. He talked about a body. As in a dead body."

Mandella dismissed him.

"You're always looking for a negative with Command Control. That's why you're on e5 and not a Hunter jet!" she sneered.

"Am I on e5 here alone?" Kaya iced back.

"I don't understand this conversation." said Triple.

"What it's all about is, do we launch the Capsule." Mandella said. "And the answer is yes. We can't ignore

212

Urth."

"You ignored Kayiga. What's special about Urth?" Kaya said.

"I won't dignify that with an answer." Mandella turned on him. "Why this chokes you, Officer Kaya, I don't know. I'll be piloting it, not you."

"Kaya, do you carry feelings for Mandella?" Sky asked.

For a moment Kaya looked awkward.

" I don't want to lose her," he said softly.

"I have no intention of being lost," Mandella reassured him.

"Me neither," said Triple.

The mood had mellowed.

"Did they bundle in a risk assessment?" said Sky calmly.

"30% survival chance," said Kaya, nodding, "that makes the Mission speculative, by any standards. They wouldn't send a baboon on 30%."

"I agree it's no moonwalk, but it's not impossible," Mandella said. "They're all pessimists at Command Centre. Remember Dogon III."

Kaya flipped.

"Me cyan listen no more to yuh stupidness, you thickskull fool!" He raised his hands in exasperation. "Now me know why dem call you Captain Disaster!"

"Yeah?" Mandella seethed.

"Lay off the Captain!" Triple shouted at Kaya.

Lieutenant Sky stepped in. "Pulses are racing. Nobody can clearthink in a rage. We have twenty six hours to decide. There's no rush. Let's each of us go away to a quiet corner and weather our heartstorms, and think." She turned to Mandella. "Captain Mandella, I think you should study the risk assessment in some depth." Then she said to them all. "Can we all do that? Find some space and reflect? We can meet again when we're all ready. If it helps, you can mail your thoughts to me, or to each other — but keep it civil."

Kaya's letter to Mandella:

I withdraw my earlier remarks. But I believe you should hold off. I cite the following reasons:

(1) Command Control have lied to us before. They should have told us about Lumpen B. They didn't. Deliberately withholding such information was arrogant and unscrupulous of them. It suggests they cannot be trusted.

(2) I do not criticise you over Planet Kayiga, but, having thought about it, I would criticise Command again. Was the destruction of Kayiga and the consequent loss of life inevitable, or the result of their carelessness? If they have been careless once, they could be careless again. We have no opportunity to check the Capsule is flight-worthy.

(3) Why us? Just as SunOne has been experimenting with black prison ships, so Command Control may well be experimenting with us. Samawitharana talks about us being his last trick. He talks about bodies, not human beings. His language suggests that the mission is doomed and he knows it. Also on this point, why have the full Ramjets not been pressed into service? The full Rams have the strength to make the Mission with a wider margin for error. Although the Capsule appears stronger than e5, it is still not, in my considered view, robust enough for the mission proposed.

(4) 30% is a gross overstatement of the mission's chances of success. As demonstrated by a cursory examination of the mathematical model downloaded by Command — i.e. Command's own figures — there is an absolute maximum 20% chance of survival. Those are very bad odds for a human life. I do not think I exaggerate when I say the Capsule has all the mid-flight manoeuvrability of an old-fashioned firework. You light the touch paper/fire the engine, and it ends up who knows where.

Finally, I do not argue any of this from self-interest. I acknowledge, Captain Mandella, that you are only risking your own life. I respect also that it is your decision, and I acknowledge it is brave of you to volunteer. Why I beg you finally not to try this mission is because I care deeply about you, Mandella. And I don't want you to throw your life away on a Command Control whim. Please think hard about these things,

Signed SonKaya.

Meanwhile, Sky was recording her thoughts on notepaper:

This thought is difficult. I love Mandella too much. I do not want her to attempt the mission. It is likely to fail. It is no comfort to me that her death would be instant. Maybe Officer Triple should be sent. His chances would be slightly higher. Command does not have the power to send Mandella on a suicide mission without her active consent. It is hard to believe she should decide to assent.

Sky shook her head, not knowing what to do, and found herself penning a poem:

Only three shifts ago, Mandella, we shared our dreams.
Your big heart under my hands, beating like mad,
We've bonded and loved through all the trials we've had
Will you throw all that away for 'Duty'?; because that's what it
seems.

That time I pumped your stomach, do you remember it?
And when I caught you bogling in Relax — you swore me to
silence!
And when I played Confessor Milla, and you begged to do that
penance!
Your singing for me when I cried as the asteroid storm hit.

You hooked me to your lifebelt when we encountered

strife
Your kicking presence on the Bridge always made me
feel strong
Can this heart and groin ache for you be wrong?
You've given Command twenty whole years: why give
them
your life?

We were going to retire and share lawyers, beds, meals,
Nibble ears, run naked in a gorgeous planetary wind.
Are all our plans now to be crumpled and binned?
Losing you — being alone forever — can you imagine
how that
feels?

But Sky knew Mandella was not one to be persuaded by
poetry, and she crossed out the poem. She chewed her pen,
trying to get into Mandella's mind, see it her way. The
captain was stubborn, unshiftable, once she had made up
her mind. It would be easier to change Command Control's
orders. Sky decided to work both ends. She would send
Mandella her poem after all — their relationship had to
count for something — and at the same time she would
comms Commander Samawitharana with a Withdrawal of
Mission Instructions Request.

With a kiss to her fingers which pressed the screen, Sky
sent the poem to Mandella. Then she commsed Command.

The Commander's Assistant said he would
communicate Lieutenant Sky's Request to the Commander.

★

Officer Triple didn't write. He saw no point in it. He knew
Mandella well enough now to know she was beyond
influence. His thoughts on the current scenario were crystal.
First, he no longer wanted to do the mission. He'd reflected
that they didn't pay him danger money and neither was
there any clause in his contract rewarding him for absurd

feats of stupidity. Bones had taken him through the model and Command Control was definitely understating the risk. Granted what was at stake was all human life on Urth, but Urth was doomed if Command Control's information was correct. So why throw Logos even one more victim? Proceeding from this conclusion to a plan of action, the best plan, as he saw it, was also a simple one: sabotage. A non-functioning Capsule would render null and void all further debate. And now was the optimum time for sabotage, Triple knew, now while everyone was dispersed. He might need Kaya's help though. Where was the rocketsman?

Captain Mandella stood at her dais watching Monitor Five. It carried a live picture of the docking port. The Capsule was in the bay there. She zoomed the camera in. It didn't look a dangerous thing in which to travel. With its shiny, purple black skin and plump, tubular body, it looked more like an overgrown aubergine. She could see the Humjet arms folded into the sides. The Capsule hood was retracted. She selected the top camera and looked inside the cockpit. The Capsule dash was simple. The far side monitor showed up a name on the flank of the Capsule. *The Deliverer*. Behind the Capsule, in a hinged perspex pod, was the pilot's heavyweight suit. Mandella selected Bay Port Control Options from the tool menu and chose Maximum Security. A cermet glass barrier rose up from the bay floor and locked into the roof, sealing off access to the Capsule. Mandella then password-barred the barrier's Manual Unlock. Satisfied, she switched off the monitor.

She reflected. She did not want to dialogue with the crew about her decision. But she remembered what Sky had requested and decided she would write something, an open message, for them to read once she had launched in *The Deliverer*:

These are just a few words, not my dying depositions. I

have no intention of dying. It is duty, not any misguided sense of heroism, that compels me to take this mission. Lieutenant Sky will certify I am of sound mind. No cloud of Thanatos palls my thinking, I have no deathwish malaise.

I signed up for the Zimbabwe Space Force knowing of the risks. Originally I captained a Hunter B attack ship. The perils which attack craft such as Hunter B face are great. Each craft faces, on average, a survival of no longer than twelve missions. We should not cling to life, nor be morbid about death. Better to face adversity with strength and as much courage as we can summon from within ourselves, and with hope. I have loved you all, in my own way. I apologise for any personal inadequacies. I know I am not an easy person to rub along with. I now write short references for each of the crew, with a view to their future professional progression and development:

Officer Kaya: Rocket technician:

Officer Kaya and myself came late to an understanding. For all its tardiness, that understanding is, I believe, deep, and soundly based. Of Officer Kaya's skill in rocketry and associated aeronautics, there can be no doubt. He also has the gift for explaining highly complex situations and computations in clear and concise language. Indeed, his knowledge extends far beyond matters technical.

The most important discovery I made of Kaya is his standing as a space griot. This shadow side of him is a side it is better to validate than to ignore. He is a keeper of African culture, a custodian of the stories of our origins, of our present, and an illuminator of our future. Like all important griots, Officer Kaya has had his clashes with authority as the records show. The entries against his name prior to this tour show him to be admired and depracated by Command authorities in almost equal measure. Praise and harsh criticism fill the reports past on him. My report, however, can only be positive. Kaya is one who, late on I admit, I have learned so much from. He has made me a more aware person, and because of that a better person, and so a better Captain. For that reason, and the others mentioned, I commend him.

Officer Triple: Surfer and Gunner:

Working with Officer Triple has been a joy and an exasperation. He was young and green at the beginning of the tour. He is still young, but no longer green. He still exasperates on occasion. Triple is a natural surfer-gunner, but the very naturalness of his talent leads to a tendency in him to neglect training. I had to pull him up several times on this. Once he understood the demands and standards I had set, he buckled down. I suspect the fault of his unpreparedness lies not with him as an individual but with a recent lowering of Cadet Ship Training standards.

Officer Triple's good humour is irrepressible. His steady supply of mimicry and practical jokes kept us all amused most of the time. His other personal qualities are strong. He is even-tempered, and now well-adjusted to spacelife. He acquitted himself particularly well during the Lumpen B incident (see log), when he showed resourcefulness, persistence and good judgment. On the downside, he does have a streak of impetuosity which he must learn to curtail, and he is sometimes too easily influenced by other crew members. Given time, Officer Triple would make an alpha star front line force Gunner-Surfer. Before then however, he must work hard on the weaknesses recorded above. He must also learn to be more tidy.

Lieutenant Sky: Communicator.

With one of the most difficult crews imaginable, Lieutenant Sky has done a superb job. She led the group interpersonal skills sessions with great empathy and a skilful, humanistic approach. She never ran or hid from conflicts. She always accepted realities. She acted at all times with selfless devotion. Hers was an immensely regenerative presence on zsf-e5.

Lieutenant Sky's skills base is wider than that of Communicator. As second-in-command, Sky successfully took charge of zsf-e5 during my temporary incapacitation (see log). She showed coolness under pressure during numerous (logged) incidents. She proved herself an accurate shot during the Lumpen B incident. Her medical skills have been maintained to the highest standard. Her behaviour at all times has been exemplary. Without doubt, Sky is the best Communicator I have ever worked with, and the kind of Lieutenant any Captain would fervently desire. I highly commend her.

★

Triple looked all over for Kaya. Ironically he found him sitting in the docking bay, in sight of the capsule, contemplating the thing. The glass security barrier was up, sealing it off from them.

"Escuche, Bones!"

"Whap'n kijana!"

Triple sat down in a seat next to the rocketsman. Kaya was looking tired.

"Listen Kaya, I have a plan."

"She already sealed it off."

"What?"

"The Capsule. That glass won't glide back. Check it. It's password-locked from her dais."

"But I didn't. You mean she-?"

"That's it. The Captain sussed you."

"Nah." *How could she? He'd never even thought of it till five minutes ago.* Triple got up, walked over to the Barrier and hit the Barrier Retract plate. Nothing doing. Damn.

He trudged back to the loading bay rest seats and plonked himself down. The two of them looked at the Capsule behind the glass.

"It looks like giant Cuba cigar." said Kaya.

"What's a cigar?" Triple said.

"Never mind."

"It looks like two large probes, cut and shut. With a pair of grab arms shafted in, and a mini satellite port."

There was silence.

"She's wrong." said Triple after a while.

"It's her decision." Kaya responded.

"It's the wrong decision."

"I know how you feel," said Kaya, "that there is a death suit." he said, pointing slowly behind the Capsule to the perspex pod which housed the heavyweight suit.

"How d'you mean?"

"It's designed not primarily to keep the person alive, but to deliver the body intact, dead or alive. Fire, explosion, detonation, nuclear impact. The suit survives, simply melts over the body sealing it." He turned to Triple. "You still thinking of flying it?"

Triple hung his head.

"How about you?"

Kaya shrugged. "I'm useless with these stiff hands."

"Think she'll change her mind?"

"On these things, she never does."

The two sat there then.

Six hours later, when Lieutenant Sky came to fetch them, they were still sitting in silence, Triple watching the air conditioning blowing out tiny specks of tile dust, Kaya watching his shoes. Sky took the scene in. It chimed with her own mood. Mandella hadn't responded to the poem or the following letter she'd written her. She had commsed Command until the irritated Assistant had chased a response herself and informed her that the Request from Command to Mandella stayed active. Sky couldn't think of anything else they could do. Now here she was.

Kaya broke the silence:

"Have you come for us?" he said to her

"Do you need more time?" It was better for the decision, whatever it was, to be taken sooner rather than later, so they could all get used to it.

"No," said Kaya, "rather get it over with."

"Yes." she agreed.

Kaya and Triple shuffled to their feet.

They gathered on the Bridge, subdued. Mandella was there already. Nobody seemed to want to speak first. Eye contact was minimal.

"All right," said Sky, "Captain Mandella, I believe you read Officer Kaya's supplementary notes on Command's risk analysis?"

"Yes."

"And that, while you respect his arguments and equations, you have not been persuaded from your earlier position?"

"That's right." Mandella didn't look up, but she shuffled her feet in that way she did when preparing to trample opponent's argument.

"Officer Triple, you didn't mail anything. Do you have anything to add to your earlier comments?"

Triple shook his head.

"Are you willing to pilot the Capsule if Mandella steps down?"

Triple's head hung lower.

"Are you?" Sky pressed.

There was an awkward silence. Mandella broke it for him. "What kind of a question is that? He won't have to. Strike the question."

Sky bit her tongue. Mandella was right to reprimand her. Yet without Triple to substitute, things looked bleak.

"Mandella," Sky's voice faltered. She choked with emotion. "Captain Mandella, did you read my appeal?"

"Yes."

"You didn't reply."

"I... I..." Mandella looked up, right at her. Sky's eyes forced her to answer. She looked at the other two crew, addressed them brusquely: "it is common knowledge here that Lieutenant Sky and myself have a very close relationship." She stepped over to Sky, put her hands in Sky's hands. "The poem was moving." Mandella bit her lower lip between her teeth to control its tremble. She felt

222

Sky's arms enclosing her. She surrendered to emotion, Sky's palms were on her lower back through her tunic material, and she smelled the scent of her sweat. Sky buried her head in her afro hair and Mandella heard the soft gulps Sky made.

The embrace ended. Mandella stepped back, the mask of professionalism returning.

"I appreciate the remarks you made, Lieutenant Sky. And I, too, treasure the memories. However you know my decision. I haven't retreated from that. It is a duty I could never with integrity avoid. Now please," she said, visibly tiring, "no more debates. Let me go into this positively."

"We accept and respect your decision, Captain Mandella." Sky said. Her voice had lost all life.

"May I ask one thing?" asked Mandella.

"What's that?" said Sky.

"That we play one last game of Netball, all of us."

"I don't mind," said Sky, smiling, putting on a face. "There's enough time."

"Is she serious?" Triple asked Sky openly.

"Are you serious?" Sky relayed the question. She was smiling weakly to Mandella now.

"Yes. We can deal with all the technical checks later. There's enough time, and some. Right now, I just want to jump some ball with my crew!"

"I'm game," said Triple. "You in, Bones?"

"Whatever the Captain want."

"Right," said Triple, "let's go jump!"

It was the strangest game of Netball Lieutenant Sky had ever played. They turned the gravity lock full off. At Mandella's insistence, it was team against team again, she and Sky versus Kaya and Triple. The competitive spirit was supplied by Triple and the captain herself. Sky and Kaya joined in, but more in body than spirit. Sky watched Mandella with curiosity. The way she charged and soared and fought every ball. She was trying to express something to them, defiant self-belief, disdain for the perils awaiting her, a contempt for death.

Triple whooped the whoops, made the plays, rumbled for the fifty-fifty's with Mandella. He looked to be having a prime joy session. But looks were deceptive. Behind the whoops and swoops, the shots and floats, he was as miserable as Sky and Kaya: Only he was determined not to show it. The idea of Netball so close before the Mission had at first freaked Triple, but now he admired the Captain for the idea. What better way to keep everyone occupied, pass the time till Launch? Triple dunked eighty eight points. With Kaya chipping in two, that made ninety against the other team's twenty six when Sky called half-time.

Kaya complained of an ankle injury and sat it out after that. Truth was, he couldn't keep up even the pretence of playing, but thought he owed it to Mandella to at least hang around. As he understood it, that, in effect, was what she wanted, all of them around her for possibly one last time. In the Netball match, Triple didn't need him anyway.

The game clock said two minutes to go. Mandella stopped and caught her breath. The game had stretched her, relaxed her and tired her like no amount of meditation ever did, despite Sky's coaching. Triple's pranks with the ball had made her laugh and forget. It was exactly what she'd needed.

The clock gonged just as Triple shot the final score, whatever it was.

"Sky, after I shower," Mandella gasped, "I want to sleep a short while. Will you issue me a tablet?"

"Will a four hour do, Captain?" said Sky.

"That'll do."

Mandella's sleep was dreamless.

They gathered on the Bridge in a show of unity with their captain before Command Control. Sky commsed using the security frequency. The Commander's Assistant came on.

They asked for the Commander. He was unavailable the Assistant told them, but he, the Assistant was fully briefed and empowered to deal with the situation. What was their decision?

Mandella spoke.

"Captain Mandella will pilot the Capsule on the Urth mission."

There was silence for two beats. The Assistant spoke into her internal microphone, and they saw her listening to a response, nodding. Then she spoke.

"The Commander acknowledges your decision, and, on behalf of Urth, thanks you. He's busy at the moment with the Southern Logos front, but he'll try to call you before Launch. You have the full mission instructions?"

"Yes," said Mandella.

"You'll need to begin manoeuvring zsf-e5 into launch position soon."

"We're about to commence."

"Good luck, Captain Mandella."

"Thank you."

The Assistant broke off the comms link.

While Triple and Kaya dealt with repositioning e5, Lieutenant Sky was assisting Mandella with her Capsule flight preparations. Sky fumbled the catheter. They were in the suiting-up room. Mandella was naked on the bench, on her back. Sky was meant to be fixing the catheter, then oiling and attaching a series of monitor suckers to her. There were sixteen monitor suckers in all, and each had to be placed in a precise position on Mandella's body. There was a chart to guide her. The monitor wires fed into the undersuit housing, and the data then travelled along a feed line to plug into the outer suit. The outer suit plugged into the Capsule's telemetry port.

"Concentrate Sky!" Mandella said. Butt naked, her voice still carried its full weight of authority. "I don't want my urine squirting around all over the suit."

"I'm sorry. Ah, I've got it now. All right, I'm starting the suckers. Number One. Here. Where's the chart? Oh, there. This might tickle, Captain. I have to spread the lube on. It's cold."

It was 1.5 hours mission time.

"Go ahead and spread. Imagine you're basting a turkey."

"I'm what?"

"Never mind. Relax. Stop worrying about me. I do that perfectly well myself."

"How can I? I'd have to stop loving you."

"So this is the big romance scene. Here I am, starkers, more wires dangling off me than a junction box and the Lieutenant's getting lyrical."

"Did you ever love me?"

"I did. I do."

"You never said it."

"I. Love. You."

Sky smiled weakly.

"I'm pestering you aren't I?"

"No," said Mandella, But her thoughts drifted elsewhere. The challenge of the Mission wasn't that there was a particularly difficult set of flight manoeuvres. It was that the margin of error had been reduced to exceedingly narrow. The calculations of gravitational pulls, mass to burn rates, warp roll, and shield tolerances formed a complex and fragile matrix. All the data and known relationships were programmed in. What was not programmable was the solar wind effect. They had only a working hypothesis based on observation of the phenomenon. Good hypotheses. Nevertheless, only hypotheses. Her life would depend on fractional real-time, in-flight adjustments. She would have to make these adjustments reflexively, while under the high gravity pressure of Ramjet light-plus travel.

The inner suit was on and zipped. Mandella walked fully wired the short distance to the docking bay. Sky held the feed line off the ground as she walked. The outer suit was being prepared by Kaya and Triple. It was a titanium and cermet-cloth mix, burnished black, and came in three sections.

Mandella climbed into the leggings with Triple's assistance. Sky slotted the feedline into the outer suit feed housing.

"Kaya, can I wear your ring?" Mandella asked on impulse.

"Sure." Kaya took off his Egyptian amulet ring and handed to her.

Mandella wriggled the ring onto her middle left finger. It fitted snugly.

"Thanks."

"*Kishana.*" Kaya lifted up the torso and arms section of the suit above Mandella's head again. She ducked slightly and wriggled into it. Kaya locked the trouser-torso seals. Then checked them twice over manually. He pulled the diagnostic kit truck forward and started the auto-check routines. When he got the all-clear from the kit, he nodded to Mandella. Only the helmet was left. After that went on, they would not be able to see her behind the uv filter headsphere screen. They would hear her only via the radio link. Kaya took up the helmet.

Sky stepped forward. Triple hovered somewhere behind her.

"Looks like it's goodbye time again." Mandella said to Sky.

Sky kissed her full on the lips, passionately and angrily. She broke off. Mandella was unflustered. After all their joint plans. the Lieutenant had a right to be upset.

Triple stepped forward, stooped and kissed her meekly on the left cheek. Then looked awkward.

"Guess you'll miss my frown then?" Mandella said, frowning, "Well, I'll be back, Officer Triple, just watch, frowning at you like I never been gone!"

Triple smiled then.

"Just hold down the flight control end OK, Triple?"

He drew himself up.

"Yes, Captain. I'll be riding with you on Vurt all the

way." Officer Triple then retreated to where Sky was checking the suit monitors on the diagnostics kit.

Kaya put down the helmet. He hugged Mandella through the suit.

She hardly felt the squeeze and the suit was too heavy for her to raise her own arms around him. He was close, his nose was almost touching hers.

"Good luck." Kaya said.

Mandella nodded. Her face clouded.

"I hear something," she whispered to Kaya, perturbed. She listened. "Do you hear that sound, Kaya, like angels?"

"I hear sister," Kaya said.

They listened together a moment. Then the singing was gone.

Mandella dismissed it. Probably a loose vent in the air conditioning. She heaved herself forward. In three steps she was alongside the Capsule. Placing one hand on the cockpit's retracted hood, she levered herself into it. It was a tight squeeze, but after plugging in the telemetry lead, and seeing the dash respond with an all-clear, she gave a raised fist 'Go' salute. Sky saw it from the kit. The hood slid into place, sealing Mandella off from the e5 world. Mandella came over on radio.

"Looks good here. Prepare for rocket ignition."

The three made their way back to the e5 Bridge and took up their launch stations, Kaya on launch countdown, Triple on flight control, and Sky on communications.

Mandella sat wedged in the Capsule cockpit. She was calm. Occasionally primitive flickers of fear shot across from the back to the front of her mind, but her higher cortex was firmly in control. Her commitment to the mission was unwavering. She examined the cockpit dash once more to familiarise herself with the controls and read-outs. She smiled as Sky began saying something soothing over the radio.

The readouts were fine, Sky noted. Battery, radio, oxygen, temperature control, breathing rate, heart rate, adrenalin soak, it all read fine.

"You're looking Go for launch," Sky radioed her, then, "keep your breathing level. I've nudged up your oxygen count just a little. If you feel in the least light-headed let me know and I can bring it down again."

"Uhuh. I'll do that, lieutenant. Good to know I'm looking good."

Sky continued watching the monitor readings. All the while she kept one comms line open for Command Control. She was hoping fiercely they'd yet come through with a Mission Recall instruction.

Kaya was going methodically through the test routines. The Capsule rockets, as far as he could observe from remote Diagnostics and Optics, were all in order. He commsed Sky. "Put me through to the Captain."

"Captain here."

"We're in position for launch," Kaya said. "The rockets are ready. Remember you're on a two stager. The first stage is liquid burn. You must reach Hum velocity before the liquid fuel is burnt, otherwise the Humjet simply won't lick. The moment the Humjet licks, the Capsule is unstoppable. It will launch you at light plus three into SunOne's core."

"So how does this thing stop?"

"When the fuel arms combust. Environmental hydrogen can then no longer be force-funneled into the engine and the process halts. The arms are timed to combust just as you hit Urth's atmosphere."

"And if they don't?"

"Faith, Mandella. They will."

"Yes, faith." Mandella replied.

Kaya continued.

"The first stage tanks will jettison at transfer from Stage One to Stage Hum. Then the stabilising fins will pop. There may be turbulence on each of these events."

"Anything else?"

"No. Follow Triple's instructions on manoeuvres during flight. OK?"

"Fine."

"Now confirm each unit is active as I call it up on your

dash." Kaya finished.

The units all checked out without cause for concern. The countdown moved from minutes to seconds. Officer Kaya kept his voice calm and even, though the tension made him hunch his shoulders.

"Lieutenant Sky?"

"All set, Officer Kaya."

"Officer Triple?"

"All set, Officer Kaya."

"Captain Mandella?"

"All set."

"I confirm we have Go for launch."

Mandella felt a small jolt as the anchors slipped off the Capsule. She tilted her head and saw zsf-e5's port fade away above her as the Capsule dropped and continued dropping. Her radio came alive.

"Ready for pre-stage one rotation burn?"

"Confirm ready for rotation burn." replied Mandella.

Kaya fired the Capsule's two rear, port small side nozzle thrusters and the Capsule rotated one hundred and sixty degrees. Triple's Vurt model Capsule made the same manoeuvre simultaneously. Triple gave Kaya the nod.

"Confirm Stage One Position Go attained." Kaya said.

Confirm Stage One Position Go attained." Mandella replied.

"Stage One Ignition. Stage One engine fired."

Mandella watched the celestial show as her Capsule nosed forward. She felt moisture on her back being instantly cooled by the suit's heat exchanger. It made her shiver.

The speed picked up. The first stage engine was remarkably quiet. Triple came over the radio.

"Prepare for bumps."

"How?"

"Keep your tongue flat down." Sky warned her.

"My tongue can't do that." Mandella chuckled.

"Light -5." called Triple with a note of urgency. "Bank left from the asteroid belt."

Mandella banked accordingly.

"Get the nose up again. Light -3"

"Fuel empty in thirty seconds. Open out thrust." called Kaya.

"Confirm thrust on full." Mandella said.

"Light -1," said Triple. His voice rose with anticipation. "Light zero zero!"

"Confirm Humjet lock-in." called Kaya.

"Lock-in confirmed." said Mandella.

"Light +.5." said Triple "Approaching critical speed... 025° yaw to starboard. Correct!"

Mandella responded at her controls. She saw the Capsule nose twitch.

"Yaw corrected," she called out defiantly. The g — force on her larynx made talking difficult.

"She's under g5 pressure." Sky murmured to Kaya.

"Countdown to first stage jettison. Two... One... Confirm First stage jettison," called Kaya.

"Jettison." Mandella said. Her radio signal was popping and cracking.

"Pulse 130." murmured Sky to the crew.

Triple gulped as the Vurt Capsule leapt forward.

"Confirm Hum stage burn activation." called Kaya.

"Confirmed." Mandella said.

"All right, hold fast." Kaya leant back from his station. There was nothing more he could do now. It was down to Mandella and Triple and the program.

He listened as Triple guided Mandella on the flight.

"Light 2. Easy now. Light 2.5. Steady incline. Light 2.7. Twist wave to port, edge the nose up .25. Easy does it." said Triple.

"Pulse 180. G at max force." Mandella responded.

"Velocity's plateau'd out," Triple reassured her. "Arc off — warp wave approaching!"

"Ar-c-ing."

"Reverse arc — counter wave ahead!"

"Re-verse con-firm."

Triple's cursed. "Slow! Hood D rings detaching!"

"Where's the dial gone?" called Sky. "Pressure gauge at

zero! Abort Mission!"

"Impossible," said Kaya, "there's no eject."

"Hood's wobbling. Still too much v." Triple called.

"SunOne event horizon at minus ten." said Kaya. Only ten more seconds to safety.

Mandella's voice came through. "It's spli-nt--ing. The ho-od. There's a—"

"Blown! Blown!" Triple cried.

"Mandella? Mandella!" called Sky.

She got no reply.

They scanned the wavelengths in vain. All trace of the capsule was gone.

Mandella had felt the deadweight of extra g's pressing on her immediately upon Humjet burn. She found herself pinned to her seat. The Capsule bucked initially, then smoothed out. But she had it under control and felt confident. Kaya's steady voice reassured her. And she knew Triple's was the best flight advice she could get. Sky's eyes would be locked on her body monitors. She had to stay calm for Sky.

At light plus 2 the tremors started. She'd thought it was her own body resonating for some reason. But a sharp splintering noise above alerted her. Defying the g-force, she heaved up her eyes. There was a tiny fracture line in the hood. Cosmic dust was collecting along the line. The line grew. It crept slowly along the hood. Mandella's own science told her that, once the line touched the hood seals, the entire hood would blow. The Capsule dash clock said she had ten Capsule seconds until Urth.

She radioed the problem.

At Urth minus Three the hood blew.

As she was sucked out of the Capsule a slow spin of memories of her time on zsf-e5 came to her mind. She thought goodbye to her beloved Sky, and to Triple and Kaya. Then, as the deathsuit began melting over her, she smelt sandalwood, and frankincense, and heard the sound of angels. The angels were nearing. They were singing. And Captain Mandella knew the song.

Appendix 1

Sky's Cosmic Haiku: Eight Early Poems

My tongue is crushed salt
The bubbler is broken
I dreamvend ice cubes.

Moonrays raise Urth's tides
tug the souls of wanderers:
There is no destination for Urth's duppies,
Just the moon's wayward pull.

Hope springs eternal;
Time eternally corrodes.

As time evolves
It shows us all its moods:
Who dreadsleeps in the moon's rays,
Blanking time's emotions?
Which black rains in the dreamsomes?
Where thin time whirls the oceans,
in an elephant dance?:

Ta ticky-tak ticky-tak ticky-tak
Ta ticky-tak ticky-tak ticky-tak.
Ta ticky-tak ticky-tak ticky-tak
Ta ticky-tak ticky-tak ticky-tak.

From Infamy to Icesleep
to Annihilation. Bad Karma
Or flawed Nation?

The teeth of a crocodile
reflect light.
The jaws of fate
Are invisible.

heartstorms
riffle the
thoughtwaves:
the wise don't kite
their hopes
in a storm.

Angels walk the spacecraft today
And garland us with light.
Which stars did they fall from?
Where in the hemisphere?
They sing of some calamity
And shiver with great fear.

Appendix 2

Sky's Tips For Survival On Space Stations And Other
Sealed Environments.

1) Go ahead cry! Curse! Punch that bag! Accept you will
have negative emotions. Fear and loathing are all part and
parcel of a space voyager's lot.

2) Be kind to yourself. Indulge yourself occasionally. Do not
set impossible work targets or standards of behaviour for
yourself.

3) Be kind to your colleagues. You are all in this together.
You will need them as much as they need you.

4) Remember to celebrate your achievements and the
achievements of others.

5) Take those tablets! They are necessary for your general
physical and psychological well-being. Remember, a space
station is a highly artificial environment. The tablets help you
adjust.

6) Beware boredom. Trouble is Boredom's wayward sibling.
Nothing saps morale faster than boredom-induced
bickering.

7) Don't try to count the stars: aspire to the possible.

8) Respect privacy. It is important in retaining a sense of the
self. From this comes self-esteem and emotional well-being.

9) Cut those toe-nails! Remember the simple things.

10) Learn other crew members' biorhythms: know which
days, and which times of day to avoid them.

11) If you smell petrol, don't strike a match! Diplomacy and dispute — resolution skills are essential when sharing sealed environments with others.

12) Always remember where in the parking lot you left your craft.

13) It is not compulsory to argue every point with the captain.

14) When pouring boiling oil over the ramparts, check first that it is your enemy below and not those on your own side.

15) Learn to let go. All things come to an end Wave your favourite project goodbye if it gets cancelled. Console yourself with the thought that you did your best.

16) Hang on to your other selves. You are more than your job. Stay in touch with the personal you.

17) If all you are picking up is noise, try adjusting the dial! A good communicator is a flexible communicator.

18) Before you take a hammer to the malfunctioning equipment, remember first — Read The Manual!

Appendix 3

Mandella's Seven Laws Of Space Station Computers
(adapted from Rosen/Asimov/The Manual):

1) A computer should safeguard the well-being of all human beings.

2) A computer should accept all human instructions unless they conflict with Law One.

3) A computer should not weigh its own emotions or interests when calculating best courses of action, nor use its intelligence otherwise than in the service of human beings.

4) When information gathering, a computer should recognise and accept the fundamental human rights to privacy and to freedom of thought.

5) A computer should not confuse its own intelligence with human intelligence, and should never rate its own intelligence as superior to that of human beings'.

6) A computer should promote the independence of human beings and should not aggrandise to itself duties which are the proper responsibility of human beings, provided always that the available human beings are capable of performing such duties.

7) A computer should not self-replicate without the appropriate human consent.

BESTSELLING FICTION

X Press Black Classics

The masterpieces of black fiction writing await your discovery

❏ **The Blacker the Berry**   Wallace Thurman   £6.99
*'Born **too** black, Emma Lou suffers her own community's intra-racial venom.'*

❏ **The Autobiography of an Ex-Colored Man**   James Weldon Johnson   £5.99
'One of the most thought-provoking novels ever published.'

❏ **The Conjure Man Dies**   Rudolph Fisher   £5.99
'The world's FIRST black detective thriller!'

❏ **The Walls of Jericho**   Rudolph Fisher   £5.99
*'When a buppie moves into a white neighbourhood, all hell breaks loose. **Hilarious!**'*

❏ **Joy and Pain**   Rudolph Fisher   £6.99
'Jazz age Harlem stories by a master of black humour writing.'

❏ **Iola**   Frances E.W. Harper   £6.99
'A woman's long search for her mother from whom she was separated on the slave block.'

❏ **The House Behind the Cedars**   Charles W. Chesnutt   £5.99
'Can true love transcend racial barriers?'

❏ **A Love Supreme**   Pauline E. Hopkins   £5.99
'One of the greatest love stories ever told.'

❏ **One Blood**   Pauline E. Hopkins   £6.99
'Raiders of lost African treasures discover their roots and culture.'

❏ **The President's Daughter**   William Wells Brown   £5.99
'The true story of the daughter of the United States president, sold into slavery.'

❏ **The Soul of a Woman**   Zora Neale Hurston, etc   £6.99
'Stories by the great black women writers'

I enclose a cheque/postal order (Made payable to 'The X Press') for

£ _____
(add 50p P&P per book for orders under £10. All other orders P&P free.)

NAME _____

ADDRESS _____

✂ **Cut out or photocopy and send to: X PRESS, 6 Hoxton Square, London N1 6NU**
Alternatively, call the X PRESS hotline: 0171 729 1199 and place your order.

X Press Children's Collection

THE DRUMMOND HILL CREW
The No. 1 Bestselling Range Of Children's Books

Set in Drummond Hill comprehensive, this series of books for 9-12 year
olds, show a group of school friends in a variety of exciting adventures.

AGE AIN'T NOTHING BUT A NUMBER
by Yinka Adebayo   **£3.99**

Remi, Tenisha, Darren, Tyrone and the other Drummond Hill pupils go
on a summer holiday to the mysterious Headstone Manor and find
themselves bang in the middle of an adventure full of GOOSEBUMPS!

BOYZ TO MEN
by Yinka Adebayo   **£3.99**

Best friends Darren and Tyrone used to be the naughtiest children in the
school. Now twelve years old, Tyrone is the model pupil but Darren
hasn't changed. He's even started hanging out with the notorious
Smoker's Corner Crew. This puts their friendship to the test. THE
MORAL: GROWING UP CAN BE PAINFUL.

LIVIN' LARGE
by Yinka Adebayo   **£3.99**

When a show-off arrives at school, Tenisha, Remi, Darren, Tyrone and
the rest of the Drummond Hill Crew all decide that he's acting too big
for his boots. It can only be a matter of time before there's TROUBLE!

These books are already HOT property. Order your kid's copies today!

Please rush me the following Drummond Hill Crew title(s) at £3.99 each		
Title	Quantity	£
❏ Age Ain't Nothing But A Number		
❏ Boyz To Men		
❏ Livin' Large		

(add 50p P&P per book for orders under £10. All other orders P&P free.)
I enclose a cheque/postal order (Made payable to *'The X Press'*) for

£ _____

NAME _____

ADDRESS _____

_____

Cut out or photocopy and send to: X PRESS, 6 Hoxton Square, London N1 6NU

Alternatively, call the X PRESS hotline: 0171 729 1199 and place your order.

Keep updated with the HOT
new novels from
The X Press.
Join our mailing list.
Simply send your name and
address to:

**Mailing List
The X Press
6 Hoxton Square
London N1 6NU**

The Dotun Adebayo Show
Every Tuesday evening
10.30pm - 1.00am
on BBC GLR 94.9FM (London)
Time to hear what you've been missing.